Good Energy Diet for Busy People

12-Week Meal Plan with 250+ Quick and Easy Recipes to Power Through Your Day

By Sophie Marigold

CONTENTS

INTRODUCTION

Energize Your Life – The Power of a Good Energy Diet

In today's fast-paced world, feeling drained has almost become the norm. Whether you're juggling work meetings, managing family responsibilities, or just trying to keep up with a packed schedule, it's easy to fall into a cycle of energy highs and lows. Many people rely on quick fixes like caffeine and sugar to power through the day, only to experience energy crashes that leave them feeling even more exhausted. But what if there was a better way to fuel your body and mind—a way that allows you to maintain steady, vibrant energy without the rollercoaster of ups and downs?

This book is designed with you in mind. Imagine yourself: a busy professional, grabbing a coffee between back-to-back meetings, trying to stay alert through the afternoon slump; or a working parent, balancing the chaos of quick, convenient meals with the desire to provide nutritious food for the family, all while struggling to find time to cook. Perhaps you're a stay-at-home parent, juggling kids' activities, grocery shopping, and household chores, feeling the weight of daily responsibilities while searching for inspiration to put something healthy and exciting on the table.

We understand the real-world challenges of modern life, which is why all the recipes in this book take just 10 to 30 minutes to cook and are made with ingredients that can be easily found in grocery stores. This makes it simple to prepare nutritious meals without spending hours in the kitchen or hunting for hard-to-find items.

This book offers practical, sustainable solutions for fueling your body and mind, no matter how hectic your day gets. With simple yet powerful strategies and recipes that are as efficient as they are energizing, we'll help you find that elusive balance—a way to eat well, feel great, and keep up with everything life throws at you so you can stay focused, avoid crashes, and bring your best self to every part of your life.

The Connection Between Food and Energy

What you eat has a profound impact on your energy levels, mood, and mental clarity. The right foods can sustain your energy, support cognitive function, and help you power through even the busiest of days. On the other hand, foods high in refined sugars and processed ingredients might give you a quick boost, but they leave you crashing shortly afterward. Moreover, poor dietary choices can lead to long-term health issues, such as digestive problems, heart disease, and diabetes.

In this book, we'll explore how a balanced approach to nutrition can provide steady, long-lasting energy while also promoting overall physical health. From choosing complex carbohydrates that release energy slowly to incorporating healthy fats and proteins that keep you full and focused, each recipe will give you tools to create meals that fuel productivity. No more midday slumps, no more reliance on multiple cups of coffee just to stay alert—instead, you'll discover how to eat in a way that supports sustained energy and resilience while safeguarding your health.

Why a Good Energy Diet Matters

Beyond just powering through daily tasks, a good energy diet contributes to a healthier, happier life. When you feel energetic and alert, you're more likely to be productive, motivated, and present. You can enjoy more quality time with loved ones, tackle your to-do list with confidence, and even sleep better at night. This book is about more than just food—it's about empowering you to live with vitality, balancing your professional and personal life without sacrificing your well-being.

The principles in this book align with the insights of Casey Means, MD, who emphasizes the critical connection between metabolism and energy. By understanding how our dietary choices impact our metabolic health, we can make informed decisions that enhance our energy levels and overall wellness. Just as Dr. Means advocates for nutrient-dense foods that optimize metabolism, this cookbook provides practical recipes and meal planning strategies that keep energy levels stable throughout the day while supporting your physical health.

Throughout these pages, you'll find practical advice, delicious recipes, and simple strategies for making energy-boosting meals a seamless part of your day.

Welcome to the **Good Energy Diet for Busy People**—a guide to reclaiming your vitality and transforming the way you eat, think, and live. Let's embark on this journey together to create a lifestyle that sustains you, supports you, and energizes you every step of the way.

IMPORTANT INFORMATION: All recipes in this book are based on one serving, but you can easily adjust the quantities by multiplying the ingredients (just be careful with spices and seasoning). The nutritional information is also per serving.

Chapter 1

Core Principles of a Good Energy Diet

In a world that often feels nonstop, energy is one of our most valuable resources. But staying energized isn't about quick fixes or temporary boosts – it's about creating sustainable habits that fuel our body and mind every day. The Good Energy Diet is built on simple, science-backed principles that anyone can apply, even if they're constantly managing a full schedule without crashing. Let's dive into the core principles that will help you maintain steady, reliable energy from morning to night.

Principle 1: Balance Your Macronutrients

Macronutrients – carbohydrates, proteins, and fats – each play a unique role in providing energy. A good energy diet isn't about avoiding any particular nutrient but rather finding the right balance for sustained vitality.

• **Complex Carbohydrates**: Carbs are your body's preferred source of energy, but not all carbs are created equal. Complex carbs, such as whole grains, legumes, and vegetables, release energy slowly, keeping your blood sugar stable and providing a steady energy source. Avoid simple sugars and refined carbs, which may cause a spike in energy followed by a crash.

• **Lean Proteins**: Protein is essential for muscle repair and maintenance, but it also plays a role in keeping you full and satisfied. By including lean proteins like chicken, fish, tofu, or beans in your meals, you help prevent energy dips by slowing down digestion and prolonging the release of glucose into your bloodstream.

• **Healthy Fats**: Fats are crucial for brain health and help regulate energy levels. Healthy fats – such as those found in avocados, nuts, seeds, and olive oil – are digested slowly, providing long-lasting energy and mental clarity. Fats also help stabilize your blood sugar when combined with carbs and protein.

By balancing these three macronutrients in each meal, you'll avoid the spikes and crashes that come from unbalanced meals and experience more stable energy throughout the day.

Principle 2: Focus on Nutrient Density

When we talk about a good energy diet, it's not just about calories – it's about the quality of the nutrients you're putting into your body. Nutrient-dense foods provide a high amount of vitamins, minerals, and antioxidants per calorie, fueling your body on a cellular level.

- **Why Nutrient Density Matters**: Micronutrients like B vitamins, magnesium, and iron are essential for energy production, metabolism, and overall vitality. When your diet is rich in these nutrients, you'll notice improved focus, endurance, and resilience.

- **Choosing Nutrient-Dense Foods**: Prioritize vegetables, fruits, whole grains, lean proteins, and healthy fats. Dark leafy greens, berries, nuts, seeds, and whole grains are especially potent sources of energy-boosting nutrients.

- **Minimize Empty Calories**: Foods high in added sugars and processed ingredients offer little nutritional value and can actually drain your energy. By choosing nutrient-dense foods, you'll provide your body with what it needs to function optimally without the crash that comes from empty calories.

Principle 3: Eat Regularly and Listen to Your Body

Our bodies thrive on consistency, especially when it comes to energy. Skipping meals or going long periods without eating can lead to blood sugar drops, leaving you feeling sluggish and irritable. By eating at regular intervals, you help stabilize your energy levels and avoid the "hangry" feeling that can come from blood sugar dips.

- **Timing Your Meals**: Aim to eat something every 3-4 hours to keep your energy steady. This could be a balanced snack between meals or simply breaking up your day with smaller, frequent meals.

- **Balanced Snacks**: Choose snacks that combine protein, complex carbs, and healthy fats. Examples include a handful of nuts with a piece of fruit, Greek yogurt with berries, or hummus with veggie sticks.

- **Listen to Your Body's Signals**: Sometimes our bodies crave energy for reasons other than hunger, like stress or fatigue. Tuning into hunger and fullness cues helps you avoid unnecessary snacking and gives you a better sense of what your body actually needs.

Principle 4: Stay Hydrated

Water is vital for nearly every function in your body, including energy production. Even mild dehydration can lead to fatigue, headaches, and reduced concentration. Drinking enough water throughout the day ensures that your cells are hydrated and functioning properly.

- **Hydration and Energy**: Water helps transport nutrients and oxygen to cells, aids in digestion, and removes waste from the body. Without sufficient hydration, your body has to work harder, which can leave you feeling tired.

- **Daily Hydration Tips**: Start your day with a glass of water and keep a water bottle with you to sip throughout the day. Aim for about 8 cups daily, but remember that needs can vary based on activity level, climate, and individual factors. Herbal teas and water-rich foods like cucumbers, oranges, and watermelon can also help with hydration.

Principle 5: Prioritize Whole, Minimally Processed Foods

Whole foods – foods that are as close to their natural state as possible – provide more fiber, vitamins, minerals, and antioxidants than heavily processed foods. Processed foods are often stripped of nutrients and loaded with added sugars, unhealthy fats, and preservatives, which can lead to inflammation and fatigue.

- **Benefits of Whole Foods**: Whole foods support stable blood sugar, reduce inflammation, and provide your body with the raw materials it needs for energy production.

- **Examples of Whole Foods**: Fresh fruits and vegetables, whole grains, lean meats, nuts, and seeds are excellent examples of whole foods that can keep you energized.

- **Avoiding Processed Options**: When shopping, look for foods with fewer ingredients and minimal additives. Instead of reaching for a packaged snack bar, consider a handful of nuts and an apple – whole food snacks like these keep your energy balanced without the sugar crash.

The principles of a Good Energy Diet are simple, but they can make a profound difference in how you feel throughout the day. By balancing your macronutrients, prioritizing nutrient density, eating at regular intervals, staying hydrated, and choosing whole foods, you're setting yourself up for consistent, reliable energy. Let's get started!

Chapter 2

The Power of Breakfast in the Good Energy Diet

In the Good Energy Diet, breakfast isn't just the first meal of the day – it's an opportunity to set the tone for steady, sustained energy. After hours of sleep, your body wakes up in a fasted state, needing fuel to kickstart metabolism and replenish energy stores. Eating a balanced breakfast provides the nutrients your brain and body need to function optimally, improving focus, productivity, and resilience against energy crashes. By fueling up properly in the morning, you're investing in a day where you can meet challenges head-on without relying on quick fixes or stimulants.

Why These Breakfast Recipes Are Ideal for Energy

The recipes in this section are designed with energy-boosting principles in mind, combining nutrient-dense ingredients that support steady blood sugar, lasting fullness, and mental clarity. Here's why these recipes are especially effective for starting the day right:

Balanced Macronutrients: Each breakfast option includes a thoughtful balance of carbohydrates, proteins, and healthy fats. Complex carbohydrates from oats, whole grains, and fruits provide slow-releasing energy, while proteins (like Greek yogurt, eggs, and nut butters) support muscle health and help keep you feeling full. Healthy fats, found in ingredients like avocado, nuts, and seeds, slow down digestion and keep your energy steady.

Nutrient-Dense Ingredients: The recipes prioritize whole, nutrient-dense foods that provide essential vitamins and minerals. Ingredients like berries, leafy greens, nuts, and seeds are rich in antioxidants, fiber, and micronutrients that fuel cellular energy production. These nutrients don't just provide physical energy – they also enhance mental clarity and help reduce fatigue.

Low in Added Sugars: Unlike traditional sugary breakfast options, these recipes focus on natural sources of sweetness (like fruit) and limit added sugars. This helps avoid the rapid blood sugar spikes and crashes associated with processed foods, allowing you to start the day with stable energy and avoid the mid-morning slump.

Fiber for Satiety and Blood Sugar Control: Many of these recipes are high in fiber, which helps slow down the absorption of carbohydrates, providing a slow, steady release of energy. Fiber also promotes feelings of fullness, helping you avoid mindless snacking and keeping you focused until your next meal.

Easy and Quick to Prepare: For busy mornings, these recipes are designed to be simple and quick, taking just around 10-15 minutes or less to make. This ensures that even with a tight schedule, you can start the day with a nourishing meal that aligns with your energy goals.

Versatile and Customizable: These breakfast recipes are adaptable to different dietary needs and preferences. Whether you're looking for a protein-packed smoothie, a comforting bowl of oatmeal, or a savory egg dish, there's something for everyone. This versatility helps you stay consistent, allowing you to enjoy a variety of meals while maintaining steady energy throughout the week.

Why Breakfast Matters in Your Energy Journey

Skipping breakfast or starting with a quick, unbalanced meal can leave you feeling sluggish, unfocused, and prone to cravings later in the day. When you prioritize a balanced, nutritious breakfast, you're fueling your body and mind with the resources they need to perform at their best. By choosing ingredients that stabilize blood sugar, nourish the brain, and promote fullness, these recipes help you approach each day with focus and vitality.

Incorporating these breakfasts into your routine will empower you to make consistent, energy-boosting choices that align with the principles of the Good Energy Diet. You'll find that starting your day with the right fuel doesn't just impact your morning – it creates a positive ripple effect, supporting balanced energy, productivity, and well-being throughout the day.

IMPORTANT INFORMATION: All recipes in this book are based on one serving, but you can easily adjust the quantities by multiplying the ingredients (just be careful with spices and seasoning). The nutritional information is also per serving.

Smoothies

Green Power Smoothie

Ingredients:

- 1 cup fresh spinach
- 1 banana
- 1 tablespoon almond butter (or peanut butter)
- 1 tablespoon chia seeds
- 1 cup almond milk (or regular milk)

- Ice cubes (optional for texture)

Calories:	298
Protein:	8.5 grams
Carbohydrates:	37.6 grams
Fat:	15.4 grams
Fiber:	11.4 grams

Instructions:

1. Add spinach, banana, almond butter, chia seeds, and almond milk to a blender.
2. Blend on high until smooth and creamy. If you prefer a thicker texture, add a few ice cubes and blend again.
3. Pour into a glass and enjoy immediately for maximum freshness.

Why It's Great: This smoothie is packed with leafy greens for a gentle detox, healthy fats, and protein from almond butter, making it ideal for sustained energy.

Berry Protein Smoothie

Ingredients:

- 1 cup mixed berries (fresh or frozen)
- 1/2 cup Greek yogurt
- 1 scoop protein powder (optional for extra protein)
- 1 tablespoon flax seeds
- 1 cup water or milk

Calories:	375
Protein:	37.9 grams
Carbohydrates:	32 grams
Fat:	8.8 grams
Fiber:	10.6 grams

Instructions:

1. Place berries, Greek yogurt, protein powder, flax seeds, and water or milk in a blender.
2. Blend until smooth, adding more liquid if needed to reach your desired consistency.
3. Pour into a glass and serve.

Why It's Great: Packed with antioxidants from berries and protein from Greek yogurt, this smoothie helps you stay full and focused through the morning.

Tropical Energizer Smoothie

Ingredients:

- 1/2 cup mango (fresh or frozen)
- 1/2 cup pineapple (fresh or frozen)
- 1 handful spinach
- 1 tablespoon chia seeds
- 1 cup coconut water

Calories:	211
Protein:	4.5 grams
Carbohydrates:	40.2 grams
Fat:	4.8 grams
Fiber:	8.7 grams

Instructions:

1. Add mango, pineapple, spinach, chia seeds, and coconut water to the blender.
2. Blend on high until smooth.
3. Serve immediately for a refreshing, energizing start to your day.

Why It's Great: This smoothie is hydrating and rich in natural sugars, perfect for a morning energy boost without the caffeine.

Peanut Butter Banana Smoothie

Ingredients:

- 1 banana
- 1 tablespoon peanut butter
- 1 cup milk (or almond milk)
- A sprinkle of cinnamon (optional)
- Ice cubes (optional for thickness)

Calories:	233
Protein:	5.7 grams
Carbohydrates:	33.4 grams
Fat:	11.6 grams
Fiber:	4.7 grams

Instructions:

1. Combine banana, peanut butter, milk, and cinnamon in the blender.
2. Blend until smooth, adding ice cubes if you prefer a thicker consistency.
3. Pour into a glass and enjoy.

Why It's Great: The combination of banana and peanut butter provides a balance of carbs and protein for lasting energy, plus a creamy, indulgent flavor.

Avocado Berry Blast Smoothie

Ingredients:

- 1/2 avocado
- 1/2 cup strawberries (fresh or frozen)
- 1/2 cup Greek yogurt
- 1 tablespoon honey
- 1 cup almond milk (or regular milk)

Calories:	339
Protein:	13.1 grams
Carbohydrates:	38.3 grams
Fat:	14.4 grams
Fiber:	6.5 grams

Instructions:

1. Place avocado, strawberries, Greek yogurt, honey, and almond milk in a blender.
2. Blend until smooth and creamy.
3. Pour into a glass and enjoy the rich, berry-infused flavor.

Why It's Great: Avocado adds healthy fats and creaminess, while strawberries and yogurt give a tangy, satisfying sweetness that keeps you energized.

Matcha Green Smoothie

Ingredients:

- 1 teaspoon matcha powder
- 1 banana
- 1 handful kale or spinach
- 1 cup coconut milk (or almond milk)
- 1 teaspoon honey (optional)

Calories:	209
Protein:	3.1 grams
Carbohydrates:	48.8 grams
Fat:	3.0 grams
Fiber:	3.8 grams

Instructions:

1. Add matcha powder, banana, kale, coconut milk, and honey to the blender.
2. Blend until smooth and green.
3. Serve immediately to get the energizing effects of matcha.

Why It's Great: Matcha provides a gentle caffeine boost without jitters, and the greens and banana add fiber and potassium for a balanced morning pick-me-up.

Oatmeal Smoothie

Ingredients:

- 1/4 cup rolled oats
- 1 banana
- 1 tablespoon peanut butter (or almond butter)
- 1 cup milk (or almond milk)
- A dash of cinnamon

Calories:	316
Protein:	9.0 grams
Carbohydrates:	49.2 grams
Fat:	13.2 grams
Fiber:	6.6 grams

Instructions:

1. Blend oats, banana, peanut butter, milk, and cinnamon until smooth.
2. Pour into a glass and enjoy this breakfast-inspired smoothie.

Why It's Great: Oats provide slow-releasing carbs and fiber, making this smoothie ideal for keeping you full and steady until lunch.

Orange & Carrot Sunrise Smoothie

Ingredients:

- 1 orange, peeled
- 1/2 cup carrot juice
- 1/2 cup Greek yogurt
- A small piece of ginger (optional, for added zing)

Calories:	214
Protein:	12.3 grams
Carbohydrates:	33.8 grams
Fat:	1.1 grams
Fiber:	3.7 grams

Instructions:

1. Add orange, carrot juice, Greek yogurt, and ginger to the blender.
2. Blend until smooth and vibrant in color.
3. Serve fresh for a refreshing morning drink.

Why It's Great: This smoothie is rich in vitamin C and beta-carotene, supporting immune health and providing a bright, refreshing start to your day.

Apple Pie Smoothie

Ingredients:

- 1 apple, cored and chopped
- 1/4 cup rolled oats
- 1/2 cup Greek yogurt
- 1/2 teaspoon cinnamon
- 1 cup almond milk (or regular milk)

Calories:	305
Protein:	14.8 grams
Carbohydrates:	49 grams
Fat:	5.1 grams
Fiber:	5.7 grams

Instructions:

1. Place apple, oats, Greek yogurt, cinnamon, and almond milk in the blender.
2. Blend until smooth.
3. Pour into a glass and enjoy the apple pie flavor.

Why It's Great: With fiber-rich apples, oats, and cinnamon, this smoothie tastes like a treat while providing slow-burning fuel.

Pumpkin Spice Smoothie

Ingredients:

- 1/2 cup canned pumpkin puree
- 1 banana
- 1 cup almond milk (or regular milk)
- 1/2 teaspoon pumpkin spice (or cinnamon and nutmeg)
- 1 tablespoon honey (optional)

Calories:	244
Protein:	3.9 grams
Carbohydrates:	58.2 grams
Fat:	3.1 grams
Fiber:	4.3 grams

Instructions:

1. Blend pumpkin, banana, milk, pumpkin spice, and honey until creamy and smooth.
2. Pour into a glass and enjoy this fall-inspired breakfast.

Why It's Great: Pumpkin is high in fiber and antioxidants, and the blend of spices makes this smoothie flavorful and satisfying, perfect for a cozy morning.

Oatmeal Bowls

Classic Nut & Berry Oatmeal

Ingredients:

- 1/2 cup rolled oats
- 1 cup almond milk (or any milk)
- 1/4 cup blueberries
- 1 tablespoon chopped almonds
- 1 teaspoon chia seeds
- 1 teaspoon honey or maple syrup (optional)

Calories:	257
Protein:	6.8 grams
Carbohydrates:	44.8 grams
Fat:	8.5 grams
Fiber:	8.0 grams

Instructions:

1. In a small pot, combine oats and almond milk. Cook over medium heat, stirring occasionally, until the oats are soft and the mixture is creamy (about 5-7 minutes).
2. Pour the oatmeal into a bowl and top with blueberries, almonds, and chia seeds.
3. Drizzle with honey or maple syrup if desired, and enjoy warm.

Why It's Great: This classic oatmeal bowl is high in fiber, antioxidants, and healthy fats, making it a perfect breakfast for steady energy and heart health.

Apple Cinnamon Oatmeal

Ingredients:

- 1/2 cup rolled oats
- 1 cup water or milk
- 1/2 apple, diced
- 1/2 teaspoon cinnamon
- 1 tablespoon chopped walnuts
- 1 teaspoon honey or maple syrup (optional)

Calories:	278
Protein:	6.0 grams
Carbohydrates:	50.4 grams
Fat:	9.5 grams
Fiber:	4.9 grams

Instructions:

1. In a pot, combine oats, water or milk, diced apple, and cinnamon. Cook over medium heat for 5-7 minutes, until the oats are creamy and the apples are softened.
2. Pour the oatmeal into a bowl and sprinkle with walnuts.
3. Add honey or maple syrup if you like a touch of sweetness.

Why It's Great: Apples and cinnamon provide natural sweetness and a comforting flavor, while walnuts add healthy fats and a satisfying crunch.

Chocolate Banana Oatmeal

Ingredients:

- 1/2 cup rolled oats
- 1 cup milk (or almond milk)
- 1 tablespoon cocoa powder
- 1/2 banana, sliced
- 1 tablespoon almond butter (optional)
- A pinch of salt

Calories:	269
Protein:	8.9 grams
Carbohydrates:	37.4 grams
Fat:	13.6 grams
Fiber:	6.7 grams

Instructions:

1. In a pot, combine oats, milk, cocoa powder, and a pinch of salt. Cook over medium heat for 5-7 minutes, stirring occasionally.
2. Pour into a bowl and top with banana slices and almond butter, if desired.

Why It's Great: This bowl satisfies chocolate cravings with natural ingredients and provides a balanced mix of carbs, fats, and protein to keep you energized.

Pumpkin Pie Oatmeal

Ingredients:

- 1/2 cup rolled oats
- 1 cup almond milk (or regular milk)
- 1/4 cup pumpkin puree (canned or fresh)
- 1/2 teaspoon pumpkin pie spice (or cinnamon and nutmeg)
- 1 tablespoon chopped pecans
- 1 teaspoon maple syrup (optional)

Calories:	268
Protein:	7.1 grams
Carbohydrates:	46.3 grams
Fat:	9.5 grams
Fiber:	3.5 grams

Instructions:

1. Combine oats, milk, pumpkin puree, and pumpkin pie spice in a pot. Cook over medium heat for 5-7 minutes, until creamy.
2. Pour into a bowl and top with chopped pecans and maple syrup, if desired.

Why It's Great: This bowl is rich in fiber and beta-carotene from the pumpkin, providing a cozy, nutrient-dense start to your morning.

Overnight Chia Oats

Ingredients:

- 1/2 cup rolled oats
- 1 tablespoon chia seeds
- 1 cup almond milk (or milk of choice)
- 1/4 cup fresh or frozen berries
- 1 teaspoon honey or maple syrup (optional)

Calories:	250
Protein:	6.5 grams
Carbohydrates:	44.5 grams
Fat:	7.8 grams
Fiber:	7.9 grams

Instructions:

1. In a jar or container, combine oats, chia seeds, and almond milk. Stir well.
2. Cover and refrigerate overnight (or at least 4 hours).
3. In the morning, top with berries and honey or maple syrup.

Why It's Great: This make-ahead recipe is perfect for busy mornings. The chia seeds add a nutrient boost, including fiber and omega-3s, for long-lasting energy.

Peanut Butter & Banana Oatmeal

Ingredients:

- 1/2 cup rolled oats
- 1 cup water or milk
- 1 banana, sliced
- 1 tablespoon peanut butter
- A dash of cinnamon

Calories:	313
Protein:	9.0 grams
Carbohydrates:	48.4 grams
Fat:	13.2 grams
Fiber:	6.4 grams

Instructions:

1. Cook oats with water or milk in a pot over medium heat for 5-7 minutes.
2. Pour into a bowl and top with banana slices, peanut butter, and a dash of cinnamon.

Why It's Great: Bananas provide natural sweetness and potassium, while peanut butter adds healthy fats and protein to keep you satisfied until lunchtime.

Cinnamon Raisin Oatmeal

Ingredients:

- 1/2 cup rolled oats
- 1 cup milk or water
- 1/4 cup raisins
- 1/2 teaspoon cinnamon
- 1 tablespoon chopped walnuts or almonds (optional)

Calories:	270
Protein:	6.7 grams
Carbohydrates:	48.5 grams
Fat:	9.5 grams
Fiber:	3.9 grams

Instructions:

1. Combine oats, milk, raisins, and cinnamon in a pot. Cook for 5-7 minutes over medium heat, stirring occasionally.
2. Pour into a bowl and top with chopped walnuts or almonds for added texture and nutrients.

Why It's Great: This simple recipe is sweetened naturally with raisins and spiced with cinnamon, offering a warm, comforting breakfast.

Savory Spinach & Egg Oatmeal

Ingredients:

- 1/2 cup rolled oats
- 1 cup water or broth
- 1 handful fresh spinach
- 1 egg (poached or fried)
- Salt and pepper to taste

Calories:	154
Protein:	10.1 grams
Carbohydrates:	16.1 grams
Fat:	6.6 grams
Fiber:	2.2 grams

Instructions:

1. In a pot, cook oats with water or broth until soft and creamy, about 5-7 minutes.
2. Stir in spinach until wilted, and season with salt and pepper.
3. Pour into a bowl and top with a poached or fried egg.

Why It's Great: This savory twist on oatmeal provides protein, fiber, and greens, making it a complete and satisfying meal.

Berry Almond Overnight Oats

Ingredients:

- 1/2 cup rolled oats
- 1 cup almond milk
- 1/4 cup frozen or fresh berries
- 1 tablespoon sliced almonds
- 1 teaspoon honey or maple syrup (optional)

Calories:	244
Protein:	5.9 grams
Carbohydrates:	40.5 grams
Fat:	9.3 grams
Fiber:	3.2 grams

Instructions:

1. Combine oats and almond milk in a jar or container. Stir well and refrigerate overnight.
2. In the morning, top with berries, almonds, and honey or maple syrup if desired.

Why It's Great: Berries add antioxidants, while almonds provide healthy fats for a balanced, make-ahead breakfast.

Turmeric Golden Oats

Ingredients:

- 1/2 cup rolled oats
- 1 cup almond milk (or regular milk)
- 1/4 teaspoon turmeric powder
- 1/4 teaspoon cinnamon
- 1 tablespoon walnuts
- 1 teaspoon honey or maple syrup

Calories:	234
Protein:	6.0 grams
Carbohydrates:	38.1 grams
Fat:	9.5 grams
Fiber:	3.2 grams

Instructions:

1. In a pot, combine oats, milk, turmeric, and cinnamon. Cook over medium heat for 5-7 minutes, stirring occasionally.
2. Pour into a bowl and top with walnuts and honey or maple syrup.

Why It's Great: Turmeric adds anti-inflammatory properties, while walnuts and honey provide a delicious, nutrient-dense topping.

High-Protein Options

Greek Yogurt Parfait

Ingredients:

- 1 cup Greek yogurt
- 1/4 cup granola
- 1/2 cup mixed berries (blueberries, strawberries, or raspberries)
- 1 teaspoon chia seeds
- 1 teaspoon honey (optional)

Calories:	377
Protein:	15.0 grams
Carbohydrates:	57.4 grams
Fat:	9.5 grams
Fiber:	10.0 grams

Instructions:

1. Layer Greek yogurt, granola, and berries in a bowl or jar.
2. Sprinkle chia seeds on top and drizzle with honey, if desired.
3. Serve immediately for a delicious, protein-rich breakfast.

Why It's Great: Greek yogurt provides a high dose of protein, while granola and berries add fiber and antioxidants.

Cottage Cheese & Fruit Bowl

Ingredients:

- 1 cup cottage cheese
- 1/2 peach or pear, sliced (or any fruit you prefer)
- 1 tablespoon sliced almonds or walnuts
- A sprinkle of cinnamon

Calories:	291
Protein:	29.9 grams
Carbohydrates:	16.1 grams
Fat:	14.4 grams
Fiber:	2.0 grams

Instructions:

1. Place cottage cheese in a bowl and top with sliced fruit.
2. Add almonds or walnuts and sprinkle with cinnamon.
3. Enjoy this simple, high-protein breakfast.

Why It's Great: Cottage cheese is loaded with protein, and fruit provides natural sweetness, making this a light yet satisfying start to the day.

Protein Pancakes

Ingredients:

- 1/2 cup whole-wheat flour
- 1 scoop protein powder (vanilla or unflavored)
- 1/2 teaspoon baking powder
- 1/2 cup milk (or almond milk)
- 1/2 cup blueberries (optional)

Calories:	242
Protein:	24.3 grams
Carbohydrates:	26.4 grams
Fat:	4.1 grams
Fiber:	3.9 grams

Instructions:

1. In a bowl, mix whole-wheat flour, protein powder, and baking powder.
2. Slowly add milk and stir until smooth. Fold in blueberries if using.
3. Heat a non-stick pan over medium heat and pour in small amounts of batter to form pancakes.
4. Cook for 2-3 minutes per side until golden brown, then serve.

Why It's Great: With added protein powder, these pancakes are a higher-protein twist on a breakfast classic.

Egg & Avocado Toast

Ingredients:

- 1 slice whole-grain toast
- 1/2 avocado, mashed
- 1 egg (poached or fried)
- Salt and pepper, to taste
- A sprinkle of red chili flakes (optional)

Calories:	263
Protein:	10.6 grams
Carbohydrates:	19.7 grams
Fat:	16.1 grams
Fiber:	7.2 grams

Instructions:

1. Toast the bread and spread mashed avocado on top.
2. Place the poached or fried egg on the avocado, and season with salt, pepper, and chili flakes if desired.

Why It's Great: The combination of protein from the egg and healthy fats from the avocado provides steady energy and keeps you full.

Tofu Scramble

Ingredients:

- 1/2 block firm tofu, drained and crumbled
- 1/4 cup chopped spinach
- 1/4 cup diced bell peppers
- 1/4 cup diced onion
- 1/4 teaspoon turmeric
- 1/4 teaspoon garlic powder
- Salt and pepper, to taste
- 1 tablespoon olive oil (or any oil of choice)

Calories:	251
Protein:	11.8 grams
Carbohydrates:	10.5 grams
Fat:	19.0 grams
Fiber:	3.6 grams

Instructions:

1. Heat a non-stick pan over medium heat and add olive oil.
2. Add diced bell peppers, onions, and spinach to the pan. Sauté for 2-3 minutes until the vegetables are softened.
3. Add the crumbled tofu to the pan along with turmeric, garlic powder, salt, and pepper. Cook for 5-7 minutes, stirring occasionally, until the tofu is heated through and lightly browned.
4. Taste and adjust seasoning if needed, then serve hot.

Why It's Great: This tofu scramble is a plant-based, protein-packed alternative to scrambled eggs, with a generous serving of veggies for fiber and vitamins. It's a filling, energizing breakfast that provides long-lasting energy.

Veggie Omelet

Ingredients:

- 2 eggs
- 1/4 cup chopped spinach
- 1/4 cup diced bell peppers
- 1/4 cup cherry tomatoes, halved
- Salt and pepper, to taste

Calories:	166
Protein:	13.5 grams
Carbohydrates:	6.6 grams
Fat:	10.3 grams
Fiber:	2.2 grams

Instructions:

1. In a bowl, whisk eggs with a pinch of salt and pepper.
2. Heat a non-stick pan over medium heat and add spinach, bell peppers, and tomatoes. Sauté for 1-2 minutes.
3. Pour eggs over the veggies and cook until set, then fold and serve.

Why It's Great: This omelet is loaded with protein and veggies, providing vitamins, fiber, and lasting energy.

Quinoa Breakfast Bowl

Ingredients:

- 1/2 cup cooked quinoa
- 1/2 cup Greek yogurt
- 1 tablespoon honey
- 1 tablespoon sliced almonds
- Fresh berries for topping

Calories:	362
Protein:	15.9 grams
Carbohydrates:	53.1 grams
Fat:	7.8 grams
Fiber:	4.9 grams

Instructions:

1. Place quinoa and Greek yogurt in a bowl.
2. Drizzle with honey, add almonds, and top with fresh berries.
3. Enjoy as a high-protein, nutrient-rich breakfast.

Why It's Great: Quinoa and Greek yogurt together offer a complete protein profile, and berries add a touch of natural sweetness.

Smoked Salmon & Avocado Toast

Ingredients:

- 1 slice whole-grain toast
- 1/2 avocado, mashed
- 2-3 slices smoked salmon
- A squeeze of lemon juice
- Fresh dill or chives (optional)

Calories:	265
Protein:	16.6 grams
Carbohydrates:	19.1 grams
Fat:	14.1 grams
Fiber:	7.2 grams

Instructions:

1. Toast the bread and spread mashed avocado on top.

2. Layer with smoked salmon, add a squeeze of lemon juice, and garnish with dill or chives if desired.

Why It's Great: This high-protein, healthy-fat combination is satisfying, delicious, and keeps you energized.

Scrambled Eggs with Spinach & Feta

Ingredients:

- 2 eggs
- 1 handful fresh spinach
- 1 tablespoon feta cheese, crumbled
- Salt and pepper, to taste
- 1 teaspoon olive oil

Calories:	306
Protein:	14.9 grams
Carbohydrates:	3.1 grams
Fat:	26.6 grams
Fiber:	0.7 grams

Instructions:

1. Heat olive oil in a pan over medium heat. Add spinach and sauté until wilted.
2. Crack the eggs into the pan, scramble them with the spinach, and add feta cheese.
3. Cook until eggs are set and season with salt and pepper.

Why It's Great: Eggs provide high-quality protein, while spinach and feta add flavor and nutrients.

Peanut Butter & Banana Roll-Up

Ingredients:

- 1 whole-grain tortilla or wrap
- 2 tablespoons peanut butter
- 1 banana
- 1 teaspoon chia seeds or flaxseeds (optional)
- A dash of cinnamon (optional)

Calories:	474
Protein:	14.4 grams
Carbohydrates:	61 grams
Fat:	23.9 grams
Fiber:	12.3 grams

Instructions:

1. Spread the peanut butter evenly over the whole-grain tortilla.
2. Place the banana at one end of the tortilla and sprinkle with chia seeds or flaxseeds and a dash of cinnamon, if desired.
3. Roll up the tortilla tightly around the banana and slice in half, if desired, for easy eating.

Why It's Great: This roll-up is packed with protein and healthy fats from the peanut butter, fiber from the tortilla, and natural sweetness from the banana. It's quick, portable, and perfect for busy mornings.

Breakfast Bowls

Sweet Potato & Black Bean Bowl

Ingredients:

- 1 small sweet potato, diced
- 1/2 cup canned black beans, rinsed and drained
- 1/4 avocado, diced
- 1 tablespoon salsa
- Salt and pepper, to taste

Calories:	356
Protein:	11.5 grams
Carbohydrates:	54.4 grams
Fat:	10.6 grams
Fiber:	16.9 grams

Instructions:

1. Microwave or steam the sweet potato until tender (about 5-7 minutes in the microwave).
2. In a bowl, combine cooked sweet potato, black beans, avocado, and salsa.
3. Season with salt and pepper, and enjoy warm.

Why It's Great: Sweet potatoes provide complex carbs and fiber, black beans add protein, and avocado supplies healthy fats, making this bowl both nourishing and filling.

Power Breakfast Bowl

Ingredients:

- 1/2 cup cooked quinoa
- 1 handful kale or spinach, chopped
- 1 egg, poached or fried
- 1/4 avocado, sliced
- Salt, pepper, and red chili flakes (optional)

Calories:	308
Protein:	12.4 grams
Carbohydrates:	27.8 grams
Fat:	16.9 grams
Fiber:	8.3 grams

Instructions:

1. Place cooked quinoa and kale or spinach in a bowl. If desired, microwave for 1-2 minutes to warm.
2. Top with a poached or fried egg and avocado slices.
3. Season with salt, pepper, and chili flakes, if desired.

Why It's Great: This protein-packed bowl offers a balanced mix of complex carbs, protein, and greens, perfect for a power-packed start to the day.

Avocado & Chickpea Bowl

Ingredients:

- 1/2 cup canned chickpeas, rinsed and drained
- 1/4 avocado, mashed
- 1/4 cup cherry tomatoes, halved
- 1 tablespoon fresh lemon juice
- Salt and pepper, to taste

Calories:	245
Protein:	9.5 grams
Carbohydrates:	28.9 grams
Fat:	10.7 grams
Fiber:	13.2 grams

Instructions:

1. In a bowl, combine chickpeas, mashed avocado, cherry tomatoes, and lemon juice.
2. Mix well, and season with salt and pepper.

Why It's Great: Chickpeas provide plant-based protein and fiber, while avocado adds healthy fats. This simple yet flavorful bowl is filling and nutritious.

Sautéed Veggies & Egg Bowl

Ingredients:

- 1/4 cup diced bell peppers
- 1/4 cup diced mushrooms
- 1 handful spinach
- 2 eggs, scrambled or fried
- Salt and pepper, to taste
- 1 teaspoon olive oil

Calories:	282
Protein:	13.8 grams
Carbohydrates:	6.0 grams
Fat:	23.8 grams
Fiber:	2.0 grams

Instructions:

1. Heat olive oil in a pan over medium heat. Add bell peppers, mushrooms, and spinach, and sauté until tender.
2. Add the scrambled or fried eggs to the veggies.
3. Season with salt and pepper and serve warm.

Why It's Great: This bowl is high in protein and packed with colorful veggies, giving you a boost of vitamins, fiber, and protein for sustained energy.

Cauliflower Breakfast Bowl

Ingredients:

- 1/2 cup cauliflower rice (fresh or frozen)
- 1/4 avocado, sliced
- 1 egg, scrambled or fried
- 1 tablespoon salsa
- Salt and pepper, to taste

Calories:	214
Protein:	9.3 grams
Carbohydrates:	12 grams
Fat:	15.1 grams
Fiber:	7.5 grams

Instructions:

1. Microwave or sauté the cauliflower rice until tender (about 2-3 minutes).
2. In a bowl, combine cauliflower rice, avocado, scrambled or fried egg, and salsa.
3. Season with salt and pepper.

Why It's Great: This low-carb, high-fiber bowl is light yet filling, with protein from the egg and healthy fats from the avocado, perfect for keeping you focused and energized.

Greek Yogurt & Berry Bowl

Ingredients:

- 1 cup Greek yogurt
- 1/2 cup mixed berries (strawberries, blueberries, raspberries)
- 1 tablespoon honey or maple syrup (optional)
- 1 tablespoon pumpkin seeds

Calories:	259
Protein:	13.5 grams
Carbohydrates:	34.3 grams
Fat:	5.1 grams
Fiber:	3.0 grams

Instructions:

1. Place Greek yogurt in a bowl and top with mixed berries.
2. Drizzle with honey or maple syrup if desired, and sprinkle with pumpkin seeds.

Why It's Great: Greek yogurt is high in protein, and berries add antioxidants and fiber. Pumpkin seeds provide a crunch and are rich in healthy fats and minerals.

Almond Butter Banana Bowl

Ingredients:

- 1/2 cup rolled oats, cooked in water or milk
- 1/2 banana, sliced
- 1 tablespoon almond butter
- 1 teaspoon chia seeds

Calories:	359
Protein:	11.0 grams
Carbohydrates:	49.4 grams
Fat:	16.5 grams
Fiber:	10.9 grams

Instructions:

1. Cook oats according to package instructions and place in a bowl.
2. Top with sliced banana, almond butter, and chia seeds.

Why It's Great: This bowl combines slow-releasing carbs from oats with protein and healthy fats from almond butter, providing a delicious and balanced breakfast.

Spinach & Mushroom Scramble Bowl

Ingredients:

- 2 large eggs (or egg whites for lower fat)
- 1/4 cup fresh spinach, chopped
- 1/4 cup mushrooms, sliced
- 1 tablespoon olive oil or avocado oil
- 1 tablespoon nutritional yeast (optional, for a cheesy flavor)
- Salt and pepper, to taste
- Fresh herbs for garnish

Calories:	290
Protein:	15.5 grams
Carbohydrates:	5.0 grams
Fat:	24.7 grams
Fiber:	2.0 grams

Instructions:

1. Heat the oil in a pan over medium heat.
2. Add the mushrooms and sauté for 2-3 minutes until softened.
3. Add the spinach and cook for an additional minute, until wilted.
4. Crack the eggs into the pan and scramble them with the vegetables. Cook until the eggs are fully set, about 3-4 minutes.
5. Season with salt and pepper, and sprinkle with nutritional yeast if desired.
6. Serve in a bowl, garnished with fresh herbs.

Why It's Great: This scramble is packed with protein from the eggs and provides fiber and antioxidants from the spinach and mushrooms. The nutritional yeast adds a cheesy flavor without any dairy, making it a delicious and filling option that will keep you energized throughout the day.

Fruit & Nut Quinoa Bowl

Ingredients:

- 1/2 cup cooked quinoa
- 1/4 cup sliced strawberries
- 1 tablespoon sliced almonds
- 1/4 cup Greek yogurt
- 1 teaspoon honey (optional)

Calories:	337
Protein:	15.8 grams
Carbohydrates:	48.0 grams
Fat:	6.4 grams
Fiber:	4.4 grams

Instructions:

1. Place cooked quinoa in a bowl and add strawberries and almonds.
2. Top with Greek yogurt and drizzle with honey if desired.

Why It's Great: Quinoa is a complete protein, and the addition of fruit, nuts, and yogurt makes this bowl a balanced, high-protein breakfast that's perfect for a busy morning.

Tahini & Berry Smoothie Bowl

Ingredients:

- 1/2 cup frozen mixed berries
- 1/2 banana
- 1/2 cup almond milk (or milk of choice)
- 1 tablespoon tahini
- 1 tablespoon granola (for topping)
- 1 teaspoon chia seeds (for topping)

Calories:	305
Protein:	7.7 grams
Carbohydrates:	40.2 grams
Fat:	17.3 grams
Fiber:	9.4 grams

Instructions:

1. In a blender, blend frozen berries, banana, almond milk, and tahini until smooth.
2. Pour into a bowl and top with granola and chia seeds.

Why It's Great: This smoothie bowl is creamy, satisfying, and packed with antioxidants from berries and healthy fats from tahini, making it a delicious and energizing breakfast.

Toasts & Quick Breads

Almond Butter & Banana Toast

Ingredients:

- 1 slice whole-grain toast
- 1 tablespoon almond butter
- 1/2 banana, sliced
- 1 teaspoon chia seeds (optional)

Calories:	279
Protein:	9.0 grams
Carbohydrates:	34.4 grams
Fat:	14.5 grams
Fiber:	8.9 grams

Instructions:

1. Toast the bread and spread almond butter on top.
2. Arrange banana slices over the almond butter and sprinkle with chia seeds, if desired.

Why It's Great: This toast combines complex carbs, healthy fats, and fiber, making it a satisfying and energizing breakfast.

Tomato & Avocado Toast

Ingredients:

- 1 slice whole-grain toast
- 1/2 avocado, mashed
- 2-3 cherry tomatoes, halved
- Salt and pepper, to taste
- A sprinkle of red chili flakes (optional)

Calories:	196
Protein:	4.8 grams
Carbohydrates:	19.5 grams
Fat:	11.1 grams
Fiber:	7.5 grams

Instructions:

1. Toast the bread and spread mashed avocado on top.
2. Add cherry tomato halves and season with salt, pepper, and chili flakes if desired.

Why It's Great: This savory toast provides healthy fats, fiber, and a boost of vitamins from the tomatoes, helping to keep energy steady throughout the morning.

Hummus & Veggie Toast

Ingredients:

- 1 slice whole-grain toast
- 2 tablespoons hummus
- 1/4 cucumber, sliced
- 1/4 red bell pepper, sliced
- A sprinkle of sesame seeds (optional)

Calories:	182
Protein:	6.5 grams
Carbohydrates:	20.5 grams
Fat:	9.1 grams
Fiber:	5.4 grams

Instructions:

1. Toast the bread and spread hummus evenly on top.
2. Layer cucumber and bell pepper slices on the hummus and sprinkle with sesame seeds if desired.

Why It's Great: Hummus provides protein and fiber, while the fresh veggies add crunch, hydration, and essential vitamins.

Ricotta & Berry Toast

Ingredients:

- 1 slice whole-grain toast
- 2 tablespoons ricotta cheese
- 1/4 cup fresh blueberries or strawberries, sliced
- 1 teaspoon honey (optional)

Calories:	162
Protein:	6.3 grams
Carbohydrates:	25.2 grams
Fat:	4.6 grams
Fiber:	2.9 grams

Instructions:

1. Toast the bread and spread ricotta cheese on top.
2. Add berries and drizzle with honey if desired.

Why It's Great: Ricotta cheese is high in protein, while berries add natural sweetness and antioxidants, making this a delicious and nutritious choice.

Egg & Spinach English Muffin

Ingredients:

- 1 whole-grain English muffin, split and toasted
- 1 egg, scrambled
- 1 handful fresh spinach
- Salt and pepper, to taste

Calories:	197
Protein:	10.9 grams
Carbohydrates:	26.1 grams
Fat:	6.6 grams
Fiber:	3.7 grams

Instructions:

1. Scramble the egg in a non-stick pan over medium heat and add spinach until wilted.
2. Place the scrambled egg and spinach on the toasted English muffin halves.
3. Season with salt and pepper and enjoy warm.

Why It's Great: This protein-packed breakfast is easy to make and provides a balanced mix of carbs, protein, and fiber.

Fig & Walnut Toast

Ingredients:

- 1 slice whole-grain toast
- 1 tablespoon almond butter or ricotta cheese
- 2 fresh figs, sliced
- 1 tablespoon chopped walnuts

Calories:	257
Protein:	7.9 grams
Carbohydrates:	26.1 grams
Fat:	15.0 grams
Fiber:	5.9 grams

Instructions:

1. Toast the bread and spread almond butter or ricotta cheese on top.
2. Arrange fig slices and sprinkle with chopped walnuts.

Why It's Great: Figs add natural sweetness and fiber, while walnuts provide healthy fats and protein, making this a nutritious and tasty option.

Smoked Salmon & Cucumber Toast

Ingredients:

- 1 slice whole-grain toast
- 1 tablespoon cream cheese or Greek yogurt
- 2-3 slices smoked salmon
- 1/4 cucumber, thinly sliced
- Fresh dill or chives (optional)
- A squeeze of lemon juice

Calories:	158
Protein:	9.2 grams
Carbohydrates:	14.3 grams
Fat:	7.0 grams
Fiber:	2.2 grams

Instructions:

1. Toast the bread and spread cream cheese or Greek yogurt on top.
2. Layer with smoked salmon and cucumber slices.
3. Garnish with fresh dill or chives and a squeeze of lemon juice.

Why It's Great: This toast is rich in protein and healthy fats, and the fresh cucumber and lemon add a refreshing touch.

Peanut Butter & Apple Toast

Ingredients:

- 1 slice whole-grain toast
- 1 tablespoon peanut butter
- 1/2 apple, thinly sliced
- A dash of cinnamon

Calories:	216
Protein:	7.3 grams
Carbohydrates:	29.5 grams
Fat:	9.2 grams
Fiber:	5.9 grams

Instructions:

1. Toast the bread and spread peanut butter on top.
2. Arrange apple slices over the peanut butter and sprinkle with cinnamon.

Why It's Great: Peanut butter provides protein and healthy fats, while apples add fiber and natural sweetness for a balanced, energizing breakfast.

Mushroom & Avocado Toast

Ingredients:

- 1 slice whole-grain toast
- 1/4 avocado, mashed
- 1/4 cup sliced mushrooms
- Salt and pepper, to taste
- 1 teaspoon olive oil

Calories:	234
Protein:	5.0 grams
Carbohydrates:	19.0 grams
Fat:	15.5 grams
Fiber:	7.3 grams

Instructions:

1. In a small pan, heat olive oil over medium heat. Add mushrooms and sauté until golden brown.
2. Toast the bread and spread mashed avocado on top.
3. Layer with sautéed mushrooms and season with salt and pepper.

Why It's Great: Mushrooms add umami flavor and nutrients, while avocado provides healthy fats, making this a savory and satisfying breakfast.

Pumpkin Seed Butter & Raspberry Toast

Ingredients:

- 1 slice whole-grain toast
- 1 tablespoon pumpkin seed butter (or almond butter)
- 1/4 cup fresh raspberries
- A sprinkle of chia seeds (optional)

Calories:	234
Protein:	8.3 grams
Carbohydrates:	23.7 grams
Fat:	12.6 grams
Fiber:	10 grams

Instructions:

1. Toast the bread and spread pumpkin seed butter on top.
2. Add raspberries and gently mash them into the butter with a fork.
3. Sprinkle with chia seeds, if desired.

Why It's Great: Pumpkin seed butter is rich in protein and healthy fats, and raspberries add a burst of antioxidants and fiber.

Chapter 3

Time-Saving Through Pre-Cooking for the Good Energy Diet

It's difficult to imagine taking a balanced midday meal to your work while you are already so many things to do or preparing a good balanced dinner when you are already worked so hard during your day. However, by incorporating pre-cooking strategies into your routine, you can save valuable time while ensuring that your meals align with the principles of the Good Energy Diet.

Pre-cooking certain ingredients—such as grains, proteins, and vegetables—allows you to streamline your meal preparation process. When you dedicate a little time to cook in batches at the beginning of the week or during weekend, you can create a variety of easy-to-assemble meals that maintain your energy levels throughout busy days. Imagine having cooked brown rice, grilled chicken, or roasted vegetables ready to go in the fridge, making it simple to whip up a nutritious lunch or dinner in just minutes.

Not only does pre-cooking save time, but it also reduces stress in the kitchen. You can confidently mix and match prepped ingredients to create balanced meals without the pressure of starting from scratch each time. Plus, with the convenience of having healthy food at your fingertips, you're less likely to reach for less nutritious options when hunger strikes.

Quick Guide to Pre-Cooking and Storing

Brown Rice

Cooking: Rinse 1 cup of brown rice under cold water. In a pot, combine it with 2 ½ cups of water and a pinch of salt. Bring to a boil, then reduce the heat, cover, and simmer for 45 minutes. Let it sit for 10 minutes, then fluff with a fork.

Storage: Store in an airtight container in the refrigerator for up to 4 days or freeze for up to 3 months.

Jasmine Rice

Cooking: Rinse 1 cup of jasmine rice under cold water. In a pot, combine it with 1 ½ cups of water. Bring to a boil, then cover and reduce the heat to low, simmering for 15 minutes. Remove from heat and let it sit for 5 minutes before fluffing.

Storage: Store in an airtight container in the refrigerator for up to 4 days or freeze for up to 3 months.

Sushi Rice

Cooking: Rinse 1 cup of sushi rice under cold water until the water runs clear. Combine with 1 ¼ cups of water in a pot. Bring to a boil, then reduce heat to low, cover, and simmer for 20 minutes. Let it sit for 10 minutes off the heat. Season with rice vinegar, sugar, and salt if desired.

Storage: Store in an airtight container in the refrigerator for up to 3 days. Best used fresh for sushi or bowls.

Cauliflower Rice:

Cooking: In a large skillet over medium heat, add 1 cup of cauliflower rice with a small amount of olive oil or water. Sauté for about 5 minutes until it reaches your desired tenderness.

Storage: Store in an airtight container in the refrigerator for up to 4 days or freeze for up to 1 month.

Couscous

Cooking: Place 1 cup of couscous in a bowl and pour 1 cup of boiling water over it. Cover and let sit for 5 minutes, then fluff with a fork.

Storage: Store in an airtight container in the refrigerator for up to 5 days or freeze for up to 3 months.

Quinoa

Cooking: Rinse 1 cup of quinoa under cold water. In a pot, combine with 2 cups of water and a pinch of salt. Bring to a boil, reduce heat, cover, and simmer for 15 minutes. Let it sit for 5 minutes and fluff.

Storage: Store in an airtight container in the refrigerator for up to 5 days or freeze for up to 3 months.

Bulgur

Cooking: Rinse 1 cup of bulgur under cold water. Combine with 1 ¾ cups of boiling water in a bowl, cover, and let sit for 12-15 minutes. Fluff with a fork.

Storage: Store in an airtight container in the refrigerator for up to 5 days or freeze for up to 3 months.

Lentils

Cooking: Rinse 1 cup of lentils under cold water. In a pot, combine with 3 cups of water or broth. Bring to a boil, then reduce the heat to low, cover, and simmer for 20-30 minutes until tender. Check for doneness and drain any excess liquid if needed.

Storage: Store in an airtight container in the refrigerator for up to 5 days or freeze for up to 3 months.

Roasted Cauliflower

Cooking: Preheat the oven to 425°F (220°C). Cut cauliflower into florets, toss with olive oil, salt, and pepper. Roast for 20-25 minutes until tender and golden, stirring halfway through.

Storage: Store in an airtight container in the refrigerator for up to 4 days.

Blanched Cauliflower

Blanching: Bring a large pot of salted water to a boil. While the water is heating, prepare a bowl of ice water. Cut the cauliflower into florets and, once the water is boiling, add the florets. Blanch for about 3-5 minutes until they are bright white and tender-crisp. Immediately transfer the cauliflower to the ice water to stop the cooking process. Let it cool for a few minutes, then drain well.

Storage: Store blanched cauliflower in an airtight container in the refrigerator for up to 5 days or freeze for up to 10-12 months. If freezing, spread the blanched cauliflower on a baking sheet to freeze individually before transferring to a freezer bag or container.

Roasted Vegetables

Cooking: Preheat the oven to 425°F (220°C). Chop your choice of vegetables (e.g., bell peppers, zucchini, carrots, sweet potatoes). Toss with olive oil, salt, and herbs/spices. Roast for 20-30 minutes, stirring occasionally.

Storage: Store in an airtight container in the refrigerator for up to 4 days.

Blanched Broccoli

Blanching: Bring a large pot of salted water to a boil. While the water heats, prepare a bowl of ice water. Cut broccoli into florets and once the water is boiling, add the florets. Blanch for about 2-3 minutes until bright green and tender-crisp. Immediately transfer the broccoli to the ice water to stop the cooking process. Let it cool for a few minutes, then drain well.

Storage: Store blanched broccoli in an airtight container in the refrigerator for up to 5 days or freeze for up to 10-12 months. If freezing, spread the blanched broccoli on a baking sheet to freeze individually before transferring to a freezer bag or container.

Roasted Beets

Cooking: Preheat your oven to 400°F (200°C). Wash and scrub 1 pound of beets, then trim the tops and roots. Wrap each beet individually in aluminum foil or place them in a baking dish covered with foil. Roast for 45-60 minutes, or until tender when pierced with a fork. Once cool, peel the skins off (they should slide off easily). Cut into slices or cubes as desired.

Storage: Store in an airtight container in the refrigerator for up to 1 week or freeze for up to 3 months.

Zoodles

Choose Your Tool: You can make zoodles with a spiralizer, julienne peeler, mandoline, or even a regular vegetable peeler.

- **Spiralizer:** This is the quickest method and produces long, curly noodles. Insert the zucchini into the spiralizer and turn the handle to create noodles.
- **Julienne Peeler:** Run the julienne peeler down the length of the zucchini to make thin, noodle-like strips.
- **Mandoline:** Use the julienne blade attachment on a mandoline to slice the zucchini into noodle-like strands.
- **Vegetable Peeler:** This will create wide, flat noodles (similar to fettuccine). Simply peel lengthwise down the zucchini.

Optional - Salt the Zoodles: To reduce moisture and prevent sogginess, sprinkle a little salt over the zoodles and let them sit for about 10 minutes. Then, pat them dry with a paper towel.

Cook the Zoodles:

- **Raw:** Zoodles can be enjoyed raw in salads or as a cold noodle base.
- **Sautéed:** Heat a small amount of oil in a skillet over medium heat. Add the zoodles and cook for 1-2 minutes, stirring frequently. Be careful not to overcook, as they can become mushy.
- **Blanched:** Bring a pot of water to a boil, add the zoodles, and cook for 1 minute. Drain and immediately rinse with cold water to stop the cooking process.

Storage: Store raw zoodles in an airtight container lined with a paper towel in the refrigerator for up to 2-3 days. If they're already cooked, use them within 1-2 days.

Tofu

Cooking: Press tofu to remove excess moisture. Cut into cubes and toss with soy sauce, garlic, and ginger. Pan-fry in a skillet over medium-high heat until golden and crispy, about 10 minutes.

Storage: Store in an airtight container in the refrigerator for up to 5 days. You can also freeze it for up to 3 months.

Chicken

Cooking: Preheat your oven to 375°F (190°C). Lightly season 1 lb of chicken breasts with salt, pepper, and any preferred spices. Place the chicken breasts on a baking sheet lined with parchment paper or in a baking dish. Bake for 20-25 minutes, or until the internal temperature reaches 165°F (74°C) and the juices run clear. Alternatively, you can cook the chicken breasts in a skillet over medium heat with 1 tablespoon of olive oil, cooking for about 6-8 minutes per side, until fully cooked.

Storage: Store in an airtight container in the refrigerator for up to 4 days, or freeze for up to 3 months.

Ground Turkey

Cooking: In a skillet over medium heat, add 1 lb of ground turkey. Cook for about 7-10 minutes, breaking it apart with a spatula, until it is no longer pink and fully cooked. Make sure to stir occasionally to ensure even cooking. Season with salt, pepper, or any spices you prefer.

Storage: Store in an airtight container in the refrigerator for up to 4 days or freeze for up to 3 months.

Ground Beef

Cooking: In a skillet over medium heat, brown 1 lb of ground beef, breaking it up as it cooks. Season to your liking. Cook until fully browned, about 5-7 minutes. Drain excess fat if needed.

Storage: Store in an airtight container in the refrigerator for up to 4 days or freeze for up to 3 months.

Salmon

Cooking: Preheat your oven to 375°F (190°C). Season salmon fillets with salt, pepper, and your choice of herbs or marinades. Place on a baking sheet lined with parchment paper and bake for about 12-15 minutes, or until the salmon is opaque and flakes easily with a fork. Alternatively, grill or pan-sear the salmon for about 6-8 minutes per side until cooked through.

Storage: Store in an airtight container in the refrigerator for up to 3 days or freeze for up to 3 months.

Shrimp

Cooking: Thaw 1 pound of shrimp if frozen and peel if necessary. In a pot of boiling salted water, add the shrimp and cook for 2-3 minutes until they turn pink and opaque. Alternatively, you can sauté them in a skillet with a tablespoon of oil over medium-high heat for about 3-4 minutes, stirring frequently, until fully cooked. Remove from heat and let cool.

Storage: Store in an airtight container in the refrigerator for up to 3 days or freeze for up to 3 months.

Bacon

Cooking: In a skillet over medium heat, lay out strips of bacon in a single layer. Cook for 6-8 minutes, turning occasionally, until crispy and browned to your liking. For a healthier option, you can also bake bacon: preheat the oven to 400°F (200°C), place bacon on a baking sheet lined with parchment paper, and bake for 15-20 minutes until crispy. Remove from heat and let cool on paper towels to absorb excess grease.

Storage: Store cooked bacon in an airtight container in the refrigerator for up to 4-5 days or freeze for up to 1 month. Reheat in a skillet or microwave before serving.

Chapter 4

The Midday Boost: Energize Your Afternoon

The midday meal, often referred to as lunch, plays a critical role in the Good Energy Diet. It's not just a break in the day; it's a strategic opportunity to refuel your body and mind, ensuring sustained energy, focus, and productivity for the afternoon ahead. Here's why the midday meal is so important:

Replenishing Energy Stores

• **Sustained Energy**: After a busy morning, your body's energy reserves begin to deplete. A balanced midday meal replenishes these stores, providing the necessary fuel to keep you going.

• **Preventing Energy Slumps**: Skipping lunch or eating an unbalanced meal can lead to the dreaded afternoon slump, characterized by fatigue and decreased concentration.

Stabilizing Blood Sugar Levels

• **Balanced Blood Sugar**: A nutritious lunch helps maintain steady blood sugar levels, preventing spikes and crashes that can affect mood and energy.

• **Reducing Cravings**: Proper nourishment at midday reduces the likelihood of unhealthy snacking or overeating later in the day.

Supporting Cognitive Function

• **Enhanced Focus**: The brain requires a steady supply of nutrients to function optimally. A well-planned lunch supports cognitive processes like memory, attention, and decision-making.

• **Mood Regulation**: Certain nutrients contribute to the production of neurotransmitters that regulate mood, helping you stay positive and motivated.

Boosting Metabolism

• **Consistent Metabolic Rate**: Regular meals keep your metabolism active, aiding in efficient energy utilization and overall metabolic health.

• **Digestive Health**: A midday meal rich in fiber supports healthy digestion, which is essential for nutrient absorption and energy production.

How These Recipes Prevent the Afternoon Slump

By focusing on balanced meals that combine complex carbohydrates, lean proteins, and healthy fats, these recipes help maintain steady energy levels. Here's how:

• **Slow-Releasing Energy**: Complex carbs in whole grains and legumes provide a gradual release of glucose into the bloodstream.

• **Protein for Satiety**: Lean proteins help you feel full longer and support mental alertness.

• **Healthy Fats for Brain Health**: Fats from avocados, nuts, and olive oil support cognitive function and reduce inflammation.

• **Hydration and Electrolytes**: Soups and dishes with high water content aid in hydration, which is essential for energy.

Tips for Maximizing Energy with Midday Meals

• **Mindful Eating**: Take the time to enjoy your meal without distractions to improve digestion and satisfaction.

• **Hydration**: Accompany your meal with water or herbal tea to stay hydrated.

• **Listen to Your Body**: Eat until you're comfortably full, paying attention to hunger and fullness cues.

• **Balanced Snacks**: If you have a long gap between lunch and dinner, consider one of the energizing snack recipes to keep energy levels steady.

IMPORTANT INFORMATION: All recipes in this book are based on one serving, but you can easily adjust the quantities by multiplying the ingredients (just be careful with spices and seasoning). The nutritional information is also per serving.

Grain Bowls

Mediterranean Chickpea Bowl

20 minutes

Ingredients:

- 1 cup cooked quinoa/couscous (see pre-cooking instructions)
- 1/2 cup canned chickpeas
- 1/4 cucumber, diced
- 1/2 cup cherry tomatoes, halved
- 1/4 cup crumbled feta cheese
- 1 tablespoon chopped fresh parsley
- 2 tablespoons tzatziki sauce or Greek yogurt

Calories:	457
Protein:	21.0 grams
Carbohydrates:	68.7 grams
Fat:	11.7 grams
Fiber:	12.4 grams

Instructions:

1. Place the cooked quinoa or couscous in a bowl as the base.
2. Top with rinsed and drained chickpeas, cucumber, cherry tomatoes, and crumbled feta.
3. Sprinkle with parsley and drizzle with tzatziki or Greek yogurt.

Why It's Great: This bowl is rich in protein and fiber from the chickpeas, with Mediterranean flavors and fresh veggies for a balanced meal.

Mexican Burrito Bowl

10 minutes - Pre-cooked ingredients required

Ingredients:

- 1 cup cooked brown rice (see pre-cooking instructions)
- 1/2 cup canned black beans
- 1/4 cup corn kernels
- 1/4 avocado, sliced
- 2 tablespoons salsa
- 2 tablespoons shredded cheese
- Fresh cilantro, for garnish

Calories:	473
Protein:	17.1 grams
Carbohydrates:	77.2 grams
Fat:	10.5 grams
Fiber:	15.6 grams

Instructions:

1. Layer the brown rice in a bowl.
2. Top with rinsed and drained black beans, corn, avocado slices, and salsa.
3. Sprinkle with shredded cheese, if desired, and garnish with fresh cilantro.

Why It's Great: This bowl combines protein, fiber, and healthy fats, offering all the flavors of a burrito without the wrap!

Asian-Inspired Tofu Bowl

10 minutes - Pre-cooked ingredients required

Ingredients:

- 1 cup cooked jasmine or brown rice (see pre-cooking instructions)
- 1/2 cup cubed tofu (see pre-cooking instructions)
- 1/4 cup shelled edamame
- 1/4 cup shredded carrots
- 1/4 cucumber, thinly sliced
- 1 tablespoon sesame dressing or soy sauce
- 1 teaspoon sesame seeds (optional)

Calories:	472
Protein:	22.5 grams
Carbohydrates:	62.8 grams
Fat:	16.5 grams
Fiber:	8.5 grams

Instructions:

1. Layer the rice in a bowl as the base.
2. Add the cooked tofu, edamame, carrots, and cucumber.
3. Drizzle with sesame dressing or soy sauce and sprinkle with sesame seeds if desired.

Why It's Great: This plant-based bowl is packed with protein from tofu and edamame, plus it's light and full of Asian-inspired flavors.

Greek Chicken Bowl

15 minutes

Ingredients:

- 1 cup cooked couscous (see pre-cooking instructions)
- 1/2 cup cooked chicken breast
- 1/4 cucumber, diced
- 1/4 cup cherry tomatoes, halved
- 1/4 cup crumbled feta cheese
- 1 tablespoon sliced Kalamata olives
- 2 tablespoons tzatziki sauce or Greek yogurt

Calories:	465
Protein:	43.2 grams
Carbohydrates:	44.5 grams
Fat:	12.5 grams
Fiber:	3.6 grams

Instructions:

1. Place couscous in the bowl as the base.
2. Add sliced chicken, cucumber, cherry tomatoes, feta, and olives.
3. Drizzle with tzatziki or Greek yogurt for extra flavor.

Why It's Great: High in protein, this bowl is both satisfying and refreshing, with classic Greek flavors and a creamy tzatziki sauce.

Roasted Veggie Quinoa Bowl

10 minutes - Pre-cooked ingredients required

Ingredients:

- 1 cup cooked quinoa
- 1/2 cup roasted sweet potato cubes (see pre-cooking instructions for roasted vegetables)
- 1/4 cup roasted zucchini slices
- 1/4 cup roasted red bell peppers
- 1 tablespoon tahini dressing (or drizzle of olive oil)
- Salt and pepper, to taste

Calories:	418
Protein:	11.9 grams
Carbohydrates:	67 grams
Fat:	12.3 grams
Fiber:	11 grams

Instructions:

1. Place cooked quinoa in a bowl.
2. Top with roasted sweet potato, zucchini, and bell peppers.
3. Drizzle with tahini dressing and season with salt and pepper.

Why It's Great: This bowl is loaded with fiber, antioxidants, and healthy carbs from the roasted veggies, perfect for sustained energy.

BBQ Chicken Bowl

10 minutes - Pre-cooked ingredients required

Ingredients:

- 1 cup cooked brown rice (see pre-cooking instructions)
- 1/2 cup shredded cooked chicken breast, mixed with 1 tablespoon BBQ sauce
- 1/4 cup canned corn kernels, drained
- 1/4 avocado, diced
- 1 tablespoon chopped green onions

Calories:	508
Protein:	38.2 grams
Carbohydrates:	63 grams
Fat:	10.6 grams
Fiber:	7.8 grams

Instructions:

1. Layer brown rice in the bowl.
2. Top with BBQ chicken, corn, avocado, and green onions.
3. Drizzle with a little extra BBQ sauce if desired.

Why It's Great: This savory bowl combines lean protein and fiber-rich ingredients for a flavorful and filling meal.

Falafel Bowl

20 minutes

Ingredients:

- 1 cup cooked couscous or bulgur (see pre-cooking instructions)
- 3-4 falafel (store-bought or homemade)
- 1/4 cucumber, diced
- 1/4 cup cherry tomatoes, halved
- 1 tablespoon hummus
- 1 tablespoon tahini sauce

Calories:	405
Protein:	14.9 grams
Carbohydrates:	71.5 grams
Fat:	11.4 grams
Fiber:	9.3 grams

Instructions:

1. Place the couscous or bulgur in a bowl.
2. Add falafel, cucumber, and cherry tomatoes.
3. Add a dollop of hummus and drizzle with tahini sauce.

Why It's Great: This plant-based bowl is high in fiber and packed with Middle Eastern flavors, making it both nourishing and delicious.

Spicy Tuna Poke Bowl

10 minutes - Pre-cooked ingredients required

Ingredients:

- 1 cup cooked sushi rice (see pre-cooking instructions)
- 1/2 cup diced tuna (or cooked salmon, if preferred)
- 1/4 avocado, diced
- 1/4 cucumber, diced
- 1 tablespoon soy sauce
- 1 teaspoon sriracha (optional)
- 1 teaspoon sesame seeds (optional)

Calories:	427
Protein:	27.8 grams
Carbohydrates:	52.1 grams
Fat:	10.9 grams
Fiber:	4.9 grams

Instructions:

1. Place sushi rice in the bowl as the base.
2. Add tuna (or cooked salmon), avocado, and cucumber.
3. Drizzle with soy sauce and sriracha for spice, and sprinkle with sesame seeds.

Why It's Great: This bowl is rich in protein and healthy fats, and the fresh ingredients make it light and refreshing.

Southwest Beef Bowl

10 minutes - Pre-cooked ingredients required

Ingredients:

- 1 cup cooked brown rice (see pre-cooking instructions)
- 1/2 cup cooked ground beef, seasoned with taco seasoning (see pre-cooking instructions)
- 1/4 cup black beans, rinsed and drained
- 1/4 cup diced bell peppers
- 1 tablespoon salsa

Calories:	534
Protein:	33.3 grams
Carbohydrates:	70 grams
Fat:	12.1 grams
Fiber:	12.5 grams

Instructions:

1. Layer brown rice in a bowl.
2. Add seasoned ground beef, black beans, and bell peppers.
3. Top with salsa and enjoy warm.

Why It's Great: This savory bowl provides a balanced mix of protein, fiber, and carbs, inspired by Southwestern flavors.

Buffalo Cauliflower Bowl

25 minutes

Ingredients:

- 1 cup cooked quinoa (see pre-cooking instructions)
- 1/2 cup roasted cauliflower florets, tossed in buffalo sauce (see pre-cooking instructions)
- 1/4 cup shredded carrots
- 1 tablespoon diced celery
- 1 tablespoon ranch or blue cheese dressing

Calories:	363
Protein:	11.4 grams
Carbohydrates:	51 grams
Fat:	12.8 grams
Fiber:	8.1 grams

Instructions:

1. Place cooked quinoa in a bowl.
2. Add buffalo cauliflower, shredded carrots, and diced celery.
3. Drizzle with ranch or blue cheese dressing for extra flavor.

Why It's Great: This spicy, veggie-packed bowl is high in fiber and low in calories, providing a tasty and nutritious midday meal.

Salads

Chicken Caesar Salad

15 minutes - Pre-cooked ingredients required

Ingredients:

- 2 cups romaine lettuce, chopped
- 1/2 cup cooked or rotisserie chicken breast, sliced (see pre-cooking instructions)
- 1/4 cup croutons
- 2 tablespoons Parmesan cheese
- 2 tablespoons Caesar dressing

Calories:	340
Protein:	37 grams
Carbohydrates:	14 grams
Fat:	15.6 grams
Fiber:	1 gram

Instructions:

1. Place romaine lettuce in a bowl.
2. Top with sliced chicken, croutons, and grated Parmesan cheese.
3. Drizzle Caesar dressing over the top and toss gently to combine.

Why It's Great: This protein-packed salad provides lean protein from the chicken and a satisfying crunch from the croutons, making it a balanced, flavorful meal.

Caprese Salad

10 minutes

Ingredients:

- 1 cup cherry tomatoes, halved
- 1/2 cup fresh mozzarella balls (or sliced mozzarella)
- Fresh basil leaves, to taste
- 1 tablespoon olive oil
- 1 tablespoon balsamic glaze
- Salt and pepper, to taste

Calories:	231
Protein:	6.7 grams
Carbohydrates:	8.7 grams
Fat:	19.6 grams
Fiber:	1 gram

Instructions:

1. Arrange cherry tomatoes and mozzarella in a bowl or on a plate.
2. Add fresh basil leaves.
3. Drizzle with olive oil and balsamic glaze, and season with salt and pepper.

Why It's Great: This light, fresh salad provides calcium and healthy fats, and the tomatoes and basil add a burst of flavor.

Kale & Quinoa Salad

20 minutes

Ingredients:

- 2 cups kale, chopped
- 1/2 cup cooked quinoa (see pre-cooking instructions)
- 1/4 cup dried cranberries
- 2 tablespoons chopped walnuts
- 2 tablespoons lemon vinaigrette

Calories:	488
Protein:	13.5 grams
Carbohydrates:	74.7 grams
Fat:	18.6 grams
Fiber:	10.3 grams

Instructions:

1. Massage the kale with a bit of lemon vinaigrette to soften it.
2. Add cooked quinoa, dried cranberries, and chopped walnuts.
3. Drizzle with more lemon vinaigrette if needed and toss to combine.

Why It's Great: This salad is packed with fiber and antioxidants, with quinoa and walnuts providing plant-based protein and healthy fats.

Taco Salad

15 minutes

Ingredients:

- 2 cups romaine lettuce, chopped
- 1/2 cup cooked ground beef, seasoned with taco seasoning (see pre-cooking instructions)
- 1/4 cup canned black beans, rinsed and drained
- 1/4 cup corn kernels
- 2 tablespoons shredded cheese
- 2 tablespoons salsa

Calories:	399
Protein:	33 grams
Carbohydrates:	32 grams
Fat:	15 grams
Fiber:	10 grams

Instructions:

1. Cook ground beef
2. Place romaine lettuce in a bowl.
3. Top with seasoned ground beef, black beans, corn, shredded cheese, and salsa.
4. Toss lightly and enjoy.

Why It's Great: This salad is a fun twist on tacos, combining protein, fiber, and Tex-Mex flavors without the tortilla.

Asian Sesame Chicken Salad

10 minutes - Pre-cooked ingredients required

Ingredients:

- 2 cups mixed greens
- 1/2 cup shredded cooked chicken (see pre-cooking instructions)
- 1/4 cup mandarin orange segments (canned or fresh)
- 1 tablespoon sliced almonds
- 2 tablespoons sesame dressing

Calories:	333
Protein:	34.8 grams
Carbohydrates:	15 grams
Fat:	14.6 grams
Fiber:	3 grams

Instructions:

1. Place mixed greens in a bowl and top with shredded chicken.
2. Add mandarin orange segments and sliced almonds.
3. Drizzle with sesame dressing and toss to combine.

Why It's Great: This salad offers a refreshing mix of flavors, with protein from the chicken and a citrusy twist from the oranges.

Greek Salad

10 minutes

Ingredients:

- 2 cups romaine lettuce, chopped
- 1/4 cucumber, diced
- 1/4 cup cherry tomatoes, halved
- 1/4 cup sliced red onion
- 1/4 cup Kalamata olives
- 1/4 cup crumbled feta cheese
- 2 tablespoons Greek dressing

Calories:	183
Protein:	3.9 grams
Carbohydrates:	10.6 grams
Fat:	14.5 grams
Fiber:	2.3 grams

Instructions:

1. Place romaine lettuce in a bowl.
2. Add cucumber, cherry tomatoes, red onion, olives, and feta.
3. Drizzle with Greek dressing and toss to combine.

Why It's Great: This salad is full of Mediterranean flavors and healthy fats, perfect for a light, satisfying meal.

Spinach & Strawberry Salad

10 minutes

Ingredients:

- 2 cups spinach
- 1/2 cup sliced strawberries
- 1/4 cup crumbled feta cheese
- 2 tablespoons chopped walnuts
- 2 tablespoons balsamic vinaigrette

Calories:	180
Protein:	5.8 grams
Carbohydrates:	14.6 grams
Fat:	11.9 grams
Fiber:	3.6 grams

Instructions:

1. Place spinach in a bowl.
2. Add strawberries, feta, and walnuts.
3. Drizzle with balsamic vinaigrette and toss to combine.

Why It's Great: This salad is light, refreshing, and packed with antioxidants from the strawberries and healthy fats from the walnuts.

Mediterranean Lentil Salad

30 minutes

Ingredients:

- 1 cup cooked lentils (see pre-cooking instructions)
- 1/4 cucumber, diced
- 1/4 cup cherry tomatoes, halved
- 1/4 cup crumbled feta cheese
- 1 tablespoon olive oil
- Salt and pepper, to taste

Calories:	399
Protein:	20.4 grams
Carbohydrates:	43.1 grams
Fat:	17.9 grams
Fiber:	15.5 grams

Instructions:

1. Place lentils in a bowl.
2. Add cucumber, cherry tomatoes, and crumbled feta.
3. Drizzle with olive oil, season with salt and pepper, and toss to combine.

Why It's Great: Lentils provide plant-based protein and fiber, making this salad hearty, healthy, and satisfying.

Roasted Beet & Goat Cheese Salad

10 minutes - Pre-cooked ingredients required

Ingredients:

- 2 cups mixed greens
- 1/2 cup roasted beets, cubed (see pre-cooking instructions)
- 1/4 cup crumbled goat cheese
- 2 tablespoons chopped walnuts
- 2 tablespoons balsamic vinaigrette

Calories:	197
Protein:	5.8 grams
Carbohydrates:	16.6 grams
Fat:	12.2 grams
Fiber:	4.8 grams

Instructions:

1. Place mixed greens in a bowl.
2. Add roasted beets, goat cheese, and walnuts.
3. Drizzle with balsamic vinaigrette and toss to combine.

Why It's Great: This salad combines earthy, sweet beets with creamy goat cheese and crunchy walnuts, offering a rich variety of textures and flavors.

Avocado Shrimp Salad

15 minutes

Ingredients:

- 2 cups mixed greens
- 1/2 cup cooked shrimp (see pre-cooking instructions)
- 1/4 avocado, sliced
- 1/4 cup cherry tomatoes, halved
- 2 tablespoons lime vinaigrette

Calories:	225
Protein:	24.9 grams
Carbohydrates:	9.2 grams
Fat:	10.5 grams
Fiber:	3.7 grams

Instructions:

1. Place mixed greens in a bowl.
2. Add cooked shrimp, avocado, and cherry tomatoes.
3. Drizzle with lime vinaigrette and toss to combine.

Why It's Great: This salad combines lean protein from the shrimp with healthy fats from the avocado, making it light yet filling.

Wraps & Sandwiches

Turkey & Avocado Wrap

10 minutes - Pre-cooked ingredients required

Ingredients:

- 1 whole-grain wrap
- 2-3 slices turkey breast (pre-cooked deli-style)
- 1/4 avocado, sliced
- A handful of lettuce or spinach
- 1 teaspoon mustard or mayonnaise

Calories:	265
Protein:	18.2 grams
Carbohydrates:	25.1 grams
Fat:	11.0 grams
Fiber:	6.0 grams

Instructions:

1. Lay the wrap flat and spread mustard or mayonnaise on it.
2. Layer turkey, avocado slices, and lettuce or spinach.
3. Roll up the wrap tightly, slice in half, and enjoy.

Why It's Great: This wrap provides lean protein from the turkey and healthy fats from the avocado, making it a quick, balanced option.

Chicken Caesar Wrap

10 minutes - Pre-cooked ingredients required

Ingredients:

- 1 whole-grain wrap
- 1/2 cup cooked chicken breast, sliced (see pre-cooking instructions)
- A handful of romaine lettuce, chopped
- 2 tablespoons Caesar dressing
- 1 tablespoon grated Parmesan cheese

Calories:	352
Protein:	29.4 grams
Carbohydrates:	22.2 grams
Fat:	15.2 grams
Fiber:	3.5 grams

Instructions:

1. Spread Caesar dressing on the wrap.
2. Add romaine lettuce, chicken, and Parmesan cheese.
3. Roll up tightly, slice in half, and enjoy.

Why It's Great: This wrap offers the classic Caesar salad flavor in a convenient, portable format with added protein.

Mediterranean Veggie Wrap

10 minutes

Ingredients:

- 1 whole-grain wrap
- 2 tablespoons hummus
- 1/4 cucumber, sliced
- 1/4 bell pepper, sliced
- 1 tablespoon Kalamata olives, sliced
- A handful of mixed greens

Calories:	205
Protein:	6.4 grams
Carbohydrates:	29.5 grams
Fat:	8 grams
Fiber:	5.8 grams

Instructions:

1. Spread hummus evenly over the wrap.
2. Layer cucumber, bell pepper, olives, and mixed greens.
3. Roll up tightly, slice in half, and enjoy.

Why It's Great: This wrap is loaded with fresh, crunchy veggies and creamy hummus, offering Mediterranean flavors and plenty of fiber.

BBQ Chicken Wrap

15 minutes - Pre-cooked ingredients required

Ingredients:

- 1 whole-grain wrap
- 1/2 cup shredded cooked chicken, mixed with 1 tablespoon BBQ sauce (see pre-cooking instructions)
- 1/4 avocado, sliced
- 1 tablespoon coleslaw mix or shredded cabbage

Calories:	340
Protein:	27.9 grams
Carbohydrates:	32.2 grams
Fat:	11.2 grams
Fiber:	5.8 grams

Instructions:

1. Spread BBQ sauce on the wrap, if desired.
2. Layer BBQ chicken, avocado, and coleslaw or cabbage.
3. Roll up tightly, slice in half, and enjoy.

Why It's Great: This wrap combines the smoky flavor of BBQ chicken with the creaminess of avocado, making it a satisfying choice.

Buffalo Chicken Wrap

15 minutes - Pre-cooked ingredients required

Ingredients:

- 1 whole-grain wrap
- 1/2 cup shredded cooked chicken breast, mixed with 1 tablespoon buffalo sauce
- A handful of lettuce
- 1 tablespoon blue cheese or ranch dressing

Calories:	330
Protein:	28.5 grams
Carbohydrates:	23 grams
Fat:	13.2 grams
Fiber:	3.5 grams

Instructions:

1. Spread blue cheese or ranch dressing on the wrap.
2. Add lettuce and buffalo chicken.
3. Roll up tightly, slice in half, and enjoy.

Why It's Great: This wrap is spicy and creamy, with a good balance of protein and fiber for a filling midday meal.

Falafel & Hummus Wrap

10 minutes - Pre-cooked ingredients required

Ingredients:

- 1 whole-grain wrap
- 3-4 small falafel balls (store-bought or homemade)
- 2 tablespoons hummus
- 1/4 cucumber, sliced
- A handful of lettuce or spinach

Calories:	269
Protein:	9.2 grams
Carbohydrates:	35 grams
Fat:	11 grams
Fiber:	7.3 grams

Instructions:

1. Spread hummus on the wrap.
2. Add falafel, cucumber slices, and lettuce or spinach.
3. Roll up tightly, slice in half, and enjoy.

Why It's Great: This plant-based wrap provides a mix of protein, fiber, and Mediterranean flavors, perfect for a light yet filling lunch.

Tuna Salad Sandwich

10 minutes

Ingredients:

- 2 slices whole-grain bread
- 1/4 cup canned tuna, drained
- 1 tablespoon mayonnaise or Greek yogurt
- 1 stalk celery, diced
- Salt and pepper, to taste

Calories:	282
Protein:	17.1 grams
Carbohydrates:	24.5 grams
Fat:	12.5 grams
Fiber:	4.2 grams

Instructions:

1. In a small bowl, mix tuna, mayonnaise or Greek yogurt, celery, salt, and pepper.
2. Spread the tuna salad on one slice of bread and top with the other slice.
3. Slice in half and enjoy.

Why It's Great: This sandwich is a simple, protein-rich lunch option with a creamy and crunchy texture.

BLT Sandwich

10 minutes - Pre-cooked ingredients required

Ingredients:

- 2 slices whole-grain bread
- 2 slices cooked bacon (see pre-cooking instructions)
- 1-2 leaves lettuce
- 2-3 slices tomato
- 1 teaspoon mayonnaise

Calories:	257
Protein:	12.3 grams
Carbohydrates:	25.5 grams
Fat:	12 grams
Fiber:	4.5 grams

Instructions:

1. Spread mayonnaise on one slice of bread.
2. Layer with lettuce, tomato, and cooked bacon.
3. Top with the other slice of bread, slice in half, and enjoy.

Why It's Great: This sandwich combines salty, crunchy bacon with fresh lettuce and juicy tomato for a classic, satisfying flavor.

Avocado & Egg Sandwich

15 minutes

Ingredients:

- 2 slices whole-grain bread
- 1 boiled or scrambled egg
- 1/4 avocado, sliced
- Salt and pepper, to taste
- Optional: sprinkle of red chili flakes

Calories:	270
Protein:	12.7 grams
Carbohydrates:	27.7 grams
Fat:	12.5 grams
Fiber:	6.5 grams

Instructions:

1. Place the sliced or scrambled egg on one slice of bread.
2. Add avocado slices, season with salt, pepper, and chili flakes if desired.
3. Top with the other slice of bread, slice in half, and enjoy.

Why It's Great: This sandwich is high in protein and healthy fats, making it filling and nutritious.

Grilled Veggie Sandwich

10 minutes - Pre-cooked ingredients required

Ingredients:

- 2 slices ciabatta or whole-grain bread
- 1/4 cup grilled or roasted zucchini slices (see pre-cooking instructions)
- 1/4 cup roasted red bell pepper slices
- 1 tablespoon goat cheese or feta cheese

Calories:	190
Protein:	8 grams
Carbohydrates:	32.5 grams
Fat:	3.6 grams
Fiber:	2 grams

Instructions:

1. Layer grilled zucchini, roasted bell peppers, and cheese on one slice of bread.
2. Top with the other slice of bread and press gently.
3. Optionally, you can toast the sandwich on a skillet or panini press for extra warmth and flavor.

Why It's Great: This veggie-packed sandwich provides fiber, antioxidants, and a touch of creamy cheese for extra flavor.

Stir-Fries & Sautés

Beef & Broccoli Stir-Fry

20 minutes

Ingredients:

- 1 cup soba noodles
- 1/2 lb beef (such as flank steak)
- 1 cup broccoli florets
- 2 tablespoons soy sauce
- 1 tablespoon oyster sauce (optional)
- 1 teaspoon minced garlic
- 1 teaspoon sesame oil

Calories:	565
Protein:	35 grams
Carbohydrates:	58 grams
Fat:	23 grams
Fiber:	5 grams

Instructions:

1. Cook soba noodles according to the package instructions
2. Heat sesame oil in a large skillet or wok over medium-high heat. Add the minced garlic and beef slices; stir-fry for 3-4 minutes until the beef is mostly cooked.
3. Add broccoli florets to the skillet and stir-fry for another 3-4 minutes until the broccoli is tender-crisp.
4. Pour in the soy sauce and oyster sauce (if using), and stir well to coat the beef and broccoli evenly.
5. Add the pre-cooked soba noodles to the skillet, tossing gently to combine and heat through.
6. Serve hot, garnished with extra sesame seeds or green onions if desired.

Why It's Great: Soba noodles add a unique, nutty flavor and a satisfying texture to this stir-fry, along with a boost of protein and fiber. This dish is a balanced, energizing meal perfect for a quick and filling lunch.

Teriyaki Shrimp Stir-Fry

15 minutes - Precooked ingredients required

Ingredients:

- 1 cup cooked jasmine or brown rice (see pre-cooking instructions)
- 1/2 lb shrimp, peeled and deveined
- 1/2 cup bell peppers, sliced
- 1/2 cup snap peas or snow peas
- 2 tablespoons teriyaki sauce
- 1 teaspoon sesame oil or olive oil
- Sesame seeds, for garnish (optional)

Calories:	430
Protein:	29.5 grams
Carbohydrates:	58 grams
Fat:	6.6 grams
Fiber:	3.1 grams

Instructions:

1. Heat oil in a skillet or wok over medium-high heat. Add shrimp and stir-fry for 2-3 minutes until they turn pink.
2. Add bell peppers and snap peas, and stir-fry for another 2-3 minutes until tender-crisp.
3. Add teriyaki sauce and stir to coat.
4. Serve over rice and garnish with sesame seeds, if desired.

Why It's Great: Teriyaki sauce adds a sweet-savory flavor, making this a great protein-packed, low-calorie option.

Ginger Chicken Stir-Fry

25 minutes

Ingredients:

- 1 cup quinoa (see pre-cooking instructions)
- 1/2 lb chicken breast
- 1/2 cup bell pepper, sliced
- 1/2 cup carrots, julienned
- 1 tablespoon grated fresh ginger
- 2 tablespoons soy sauce
- 1 teaspoon sesame oil or olive oil

Calories:	480
Protein:	35 grams
Carbohydrates:	45 grams
Fat:	15 grams
Fiber:	7 grams

Instructions:

1. Heat sesame oil in a large skillet or wok over medium-high heat. Add grated ginger and chicken strips, and stir-fry for 4-5 minutes until the chicken is mostly cooked.
2. Add the bell pepper and carrots to the skillet, and continue to stir-fry for another 3-4 minutes until the vegetables are tender-crisp.
3. Pour in the soy sauce and stir well to coat the chicken and vegetables evenly.
4. Serve the stir-fry over the pre-cooked quinoa.

Why It's Great: This stir-fry has a light, fresh flavor, with ginger adding an anti-inflammatory boost and enhancing digestion.

Vegetable Fried Rice

15 minutes - Precooked ingredients required

Ingredients:

- 1 cup cooked jasmine or brown rice (see pre-cooking instructions)
- 1/4 cup peas
- 1/4 cup diced carrots
- 1 egg, lightly beaten
- 1 tablespoon soy sauce
- 1 teaspoon sesame oil or olive oil
- 1 green onion, sliced

Calories:	447
Protein:	13.2 grams
Carbohydrates:	55.1 grams
Fat:	19.5 grams
Fiber:	4.1 grams

Instructions:

1. Heat oil in a skillet over medium heat. Add peas and carrots, and stir-fry for 2-3 minutes until softened.
2. Push the veggies to one side, and pour the beaten egg on the other side; scramble until cooked.
3. Add rice and soy sauce, stirring everything together for another 2-3 minutes until well combined.
4. Top with sliced green onion and serve.

Why It's Great: Fried rice is versatile and packed with flavor, plus it's an easy way to add protein, fiber, and veggies in one dish.

Cashew Chicken Stir-Fry with Cauliflower Rice

20 minutes

Ingredients:

- 1 cup cauliflower rice (see pre-cooking instructions)
- 1/2 lb chicken breast
- 1/2 cup bell peppers, diced
- 1/4 cup cashews
- 2 tablespoons soy sauce
- 1 teaspoon olive or sesame oil

Calories:	450
Protein:	32 grams
Carbohydrates:	22 grams
Fat:	26 grams
Fiber:	4 grams

Instructions:

1. Heat the olive or sesame oil in a large skillet or wok over medium-high heat. Add the chicken pieces and cook for about 5-7 minutes until they are fully cooked and browned, stirring occasionally.
2. Cook cauliflower rice in the same time
3. Add the diced bell peppers and cashews to the skillet, and cook for another 3-4 minutes until the bell peppers are slightly tender.
4. Pour in the soy sauce, and stir well to coat the chicken and vegetables evenly.
5. Serve the stir-fry over the cauliflower rice.

Why It's Great: This dish combines lean protein with healthy fats from cashews, making it both filling and delicious.

Mushroom & Spinach Sauté

20 minutes

Ingredients:

- 1 cup quinoa or rice
- 1 cup sliced mushrooms
- 2 cups spinach
- 1 clove garlic, minced
- 1 tablespoon olive oil
- Salt and pepper, to taste

Calories:	374
Protein:	12.3 grams
Carbohydrates:	44.9 grams
Fat:	17.5 grams
Fiber:	7.6 grams

Instructions:

1. Cook quinoa or rice (see pre-cooking instructions)
2. Heat olive oil in a skillet over medium heat.
3. Add garlic and mushrooms; sauté for 5-6 minutes until mushrooms are golden.
4. Add spinach and cook for another 1-2 minutes until wilted.
5. Season with salt and pepper and serve over quinoa or rice.

Why It's Great: This light and nutritious sauté is rich in fiber, vitamins, and antioxidants, making it perfect for a healthy, low-calorie lunch.

Garlic Shrimp & Asparagus

25 minutes

Ingredients:

- 1 cup quinoa or rice
- 1/2 lb shrimp,
- 1/2 cup asparagus, trimmed and cut into 1-inch pieces
- 2 cloves garlic, minced
- 1 tablespoon olive oil
- Salt and pepper, to taste
- Lemon wedge (optional)

Calories:	410
Protein:	28 grams
Carbohydrates:	42 grams
Fat:	14 grams
Fiber:	5 grams

Instructions:

1. Heat olive oil in a skillet over medium-high heat. Add garlic and cook for about 30 seconds until fragrant.
2. Add shrimp and cook for 2-3 minutes until they turn pink and opaque.
3. Add asparagus and sauté for another 2-3 minutes until tender-crisp. Season with salt and pepper to taste.
4. Serve over quinoa or rice, and garnish with a squeeze of lemon if desired.

Why It's Great: This dish is high in lean protein from the shrimp and packed with vitamins from the asparagus, making it light yet satisfying.

Tofu & Veggie Stir-Fry with Zoodles

20 minutes

Ingredients:

- 1 cup zucchini noodles (zoodles), see pre-cooking instructions
- 1/2 block firm tofu, cubed
- 1/2 cup broccoli florets
- 1/4 cup bell pepper, sliced
- 2 tablespoons soy sauce
- 1 teaspoon sesame oil

Calories:	220
Protein:	12 grams
Carbohydrates:	12 grams
Fat:	15 grams
Fiber:	4 grams

Instructions:

1. Heat the sesame oil in a large skillet or wok over medium-high heat. Add the cubed tofu and cook for 3-4 minutes, turning occasionally until the tofu is golden and crisp on all sides. Remove the tofu from the skillet and set aside.
2. In the same skillet, add the broccoli and bell pepper. Sauté for 3-5 minutes, or until the vegetables are tender-crisp.
3. Add the tofu back to the skillet, along with the soy sauce. Stir well to coat the ingredients evenly.
4. Add the zoodles to the skillet and stir-fry for an additional 1-2 minutes, just until the zucchini noodles are warmed but still firm (they will soften quickly).
5. Serve immediately

Why It's Great: Zoodles are a low-carb, fiber-rich alternative to traditional noodles, making this stir-fry lighter while adding a fresh crunch and vibrant color. This dish is a great balance of plant-based protein, fiber, and essential nutrients.

Beef & Bell Pepper Stir-Fry

20 minutes

Ingredients:

- 1 cup sweet potato noodles
- 1/2 lb beef (such as flank or sirloin steak), thinly sliced
- 1/2 cup red bell pepper, sliced
- 1/2 cup green bell pepper, sliced
- 2 tablespoons soy sauce
- 1 teaspoon sesame oil or olive oil
- 1 clove garlic, minced
- 1/2 teaspoon grated fresh ginger (optional)

Calories:	435
Protein:	28 grams
Carbohydrates:	25 grams
Fat:	25 grams
Fiber:	4 grams

Instructions:

1. If using raw noodles, blanch them in boiling water for about 1-2 minutes to soften slightly, then drain. Alternatively, you can sauté them in a skillet with a little olive oil for 3-4 minutes until tender but not mushy.
2. Heat sesame oil in a large skillet or wok over medium-high heat.
3. Add garlic (and ginger, if using) and sliced beef. Stir-fry for 3-4 minutes until the beef is mostly cooked.
4. Add red and green bell peppers to the skillet, and stir-fry for another 3-4 minutes until the peppers are tender-crisp.
5. Pour in soy sauce and stir to coat the beef and vegetables evenly.
6. Add the blanched or sautéed sweet potato noodles to the skillet, tossing gently to combine with the beef and vegetables.
7. Serve immediately, garnished with additional sesame seeds or fresh herbs if desired.

Why It's Great: Sweet potato noodles add a subtle sweetness and a nutrient-rich base to the dish, complementing the savory beef and peppers. High in vitamins A and C, sweet potato noodles provide a healthy, energy-boosting alternative to traditional rice.

Zucchini & Chickpea Sauté

20 minutes

Ingredients:

- 1 cup quinoa or couscous
- 1/2 zucchini, sliced into half-moons
- 1/2 cup canned chickpeas, rinsed and drained
- 1/4 cup cherry tomatoes, halved
- 1 tablespoon olive oil
- Salt and pepper, to taste
- Fresh basil or parsley, for garnish

Calories:	425
Protein:	13 grams
Carbohydrates:	54 grams
Fat:	16 grams
Fiber:	9 grams

Instructions:

1. Cook quinoa or couscous (see pre-cooking instructions)
2. Heat olive oil in a skillet over medium heat.
3. Add zucchini and sauté for 4-5 minutes until golden and tender.
4. Add chickpeas and cherry tomatoes, and cook for another 2-3 minutes until warmed through.
5. Season with salt and pepper, and garnish with fresh herbs.
6. Serve over quinoa or couscous.

Why It's Great: This light, veggie-packed dish is filled with fiber, plant-based protein, and fresh flavors, perfect for a quick and nutritious lunch.

Pasta & Noodle Dishes

Pasta Primavera

20 minutes

Ingredients:

- 1 cup pasta
- 1/4 cup cherry tomatoes, halved
- 1/4 cup zucchini, sliced
- 1/4 cup bell pepper, diced
- 1 tablespoon olive oil
- 1 clove garlic, minced
- Salt and pepper, to taste
- Fresh basil or parsley, for garnish
- Grated Parmesan, for serving (optional)

Calories:	400
Protein:	10 grams
Carbohydrates:	60 grams
Fat:	13 grams
Fiber:	5 grams

Instructions:

1. Cook pasta according to package instructions.
2. Heat olive oil in a skillet over medium heat.
3. Add garlic, zucchini, and bell pepper; sauté for 3-4 minutes until veggies are tender.
4. Add cherry tomatoes and cooked pasta; toss to combine and heat through.
5. Season with salt and pepper, garnish with fresh herbs and Parmesan, if desired, and serve.

Why It's Great: This dish provides a balanced mix of complex carbohydrates, fiber, and healthy fats, with the option for added protein and flavor from Parmesan cheese. The fresh vegetables add color, nutrients, and flavor to the pasta, making it a light yet satisfying meal.

Garlic Shrimp Pasta

15 minutes

Ingredients:

- 1 cup pasta (such as spaghetti or linguine)
- 1/2 lb shrimp, peeled and deveined
- 2 cloves garlic, minced
- 1 tablespoon olive oil or butter
- Salt and pepper, to taste
- Fresh parsley, for garnish
- Lemon wedge (optional)

Calories:	520
Protein:	30 grams
Carbohydrates:	60 grams
Fat:	18 grams
Fiber:	3 grams

Instructions:

1. Cook pasta according to package instructions.
2. Heat olive oil or butter in a skillet over medium heat.
3. Add garlic and shrimp; sauté for 2-3 minutes until shrimp turn pink and opaque.
4. Add the cooked pasta and toss to combine, heating through.
5. Season with salt and pepper, garnish with parsley, and serve with a squeeze of lemon.

Why It's Great: This pasta dish offers a good balance of protein from the shrimp and energy-sustaining carbohydrates from the pasta.

Pesto Chicken Pasta

20 minutes

Ingredients:

- 1 cup pasta (penne or fusilli)
- 1/2 cup cooked chicken breast (see pre-cooking instructions)
- 2 tablespoons pesto sauce
- 1/4 cup cherry tomatoes, halved
- Salt and pepper, to taste
- Grated Parmesan (optional)

Calories:	480
Protein:	28 grams
Carbohydrates:	52 grams
Fat:	18 grams
Fiber:	4 grams

Instructions:

1. Cook pasta according to package instructions.
2. Combine cooked pasta, sliced chicken, and pesto sauce in a skillet over medium heat.
3. Add cherry tomatoes and toss to coat, heating through.
4. Season with salt and pepper, and garnish with Parmesan if desired.

Why It's Great: This dish combines protein-rich chicken with flavorful pesto and energy-sustaining pasta, making it a well-rounded meal.

Peanut Noodles

15 minutes

Ingredients:

- 1 cup rice noodles
- 1/4 cup bell pepper, sliced
- 1/4 cup cucumber, julienned
- 1/4 cup shredded carrots
- 2 tablespoons peanut sauce
- 1 tablespoon chopped peanuts
- Fresh cilantro (optional)

Calories:	420
Protein:	9 grams
Carbohydrates:	66 grams
Fat:	15 grams
Fiber:	4 grams

Instructions:

1. Cook rice noodles according to package instructions, drain, and rinse with cold water. Toss with a bit of oil to prevent sticking.
2. Combine cooked rice noodles, bell pepper, cucumber, and shredded carrots in a bowl.
3. Drizzle with peanut sauce and toss to coat.
4. Garnish with chopped peanuts and fresh cilantro, if desired.

Why It's Great: This dish is a quick, plant-based option that provides energy-sustaining carbohydrates from the rice noodles and healthy fats from the peanuts.

Tomato Basil Pasta

15 minutes

Ingredients:

- 1 cup pasta (penne or spaghetti)
- 1/2 cup cherry tomatoes, halved
- 1 tablespoon olive oil
- 1 clove garlic, minced
- Fresh basil, torn
- Salt and pepper, to taste
- Grated Parmesan (optional)

Calories:	400
Protein:	11 grams
Carbohydrates:	62 grams
Fat:	11 grams
Fiber:	4 grams

Instructions:

1. Cook pasta according to package instructions.
2. Heat olive oil in a skillet over medium heat. Add garlic and cherry tomatoes, and sauté for 2-3 minutes until tomatoes are softened.
3. Add cooked pasta and toss to combine, heating through.
4. Season with salt and pepper, garnish with fresh basil and Parmesan if desired, and serve.

Why It's Great: This light, fresh pasta is packed with the simple flavors of tomatoes and basil, making it a perfect summer meal.

Broccoli & Chicken Alfredo

20 minutes

Ingredients:

- 1 cup pasta (such as fettuccine)
- 1/2 cup cooked chicken breast (see pre-cooking instructions)
- 1/2 cup broccoli florets (see pre-cooking instructions)
- 1/4 cup Alfredo sauce (store-bought or homemade)
- Grated Parmesan (optional)

Calories:	520
Protein:	28 grams
Carbohydrates:	62 grams
Fat:	18 grams
Fiber:	5 grams

Instructions:

1. Cook pasta according to package instructions. Blanch broccoli (see pre-cooking instructions).
2. Combine cooked pasta, chicken, and blanched broccoli in a skillet over medium heat.
3. Add Alfredo sauce and toss to coat, heating through.
4. Garnish with Parmesan if desired and serve.

Why It's Great: This dish provides a creamy, comforting flavor with added nutrients from the broccoli, making it both indulgent and healthy.

Zoodles with Marinara

15 minutes

Ingredients:

- 1 cup zucchini noodles (zoodles), see pre-cooking instructions
- 1/2 cup marinara sauce (store-bought or homemade)
- Salt and pepper, to taste
- Grated Parmesan, for serving (optional)

Calories:	120
Protein:	3 grams
Carbohydrates:	16 grams
Fat:	5 grams
Fiber:	4 grams

Instructions:

1. In a skillet, heat a tablespoon of olive oil over medium heat. Add the zucchini noodles and sauté for about 3-5 minutes, tossing gently until they are tender but still slightly firm.
2. Heat marinara sauce in a skillet over medium heat.
3. Add zoodles and toss to coat, cooking for 2-3 minutes until warmed through.
4. Season with salt and pepper, and garnish with Parmesan if desired.

Why It's Great: This low-carb option offers a fresh and light alternative to traditional pasta, with all the comforting flavor of marinara.

Spicy Beef Ramen

15 minutes

Ingredients:

- 1 package ramen noodles
- 1/2 cup ground beef
- 1/2 cup spinach
- 1 green onion, sliced
- 1 teaspoon sriracha or chili paste
- 1 teaspoon sesame oil

Calories:	480
Protein:	20 grams
Carbohydrates:	45 grams
Fat:	24 grams
Fiber:	3 grams

Instructions:

1. Cook ramen according to package instructions.
2. Heat sesame oil in a skillet over medium heat.
3. Cook sliced ground beef with salt and pepper (see pre-cooking instructions)
4. Add cooked ramen noodles, spinach, and sriracha or chili paste; toss to combine and heat through until spinach wilts.
5. Top with sliced green onions and serve.

Why It's Great: This flavorful and spicy ramen is a quick, satisfying meal that combines protein from the beef with the vibrant flavors of sesame oil and sriracha. The spinach adds a nutrient boost, and the ramen noodles provide energy-sustaining carbohydrates.

Lemon Garlic Shrimp Linguine

20 minutes

Ingredients:

- 1 cup linguine
- 1/2 lb shrimp
- 2 cloves garlic, minced
- 1 tablespoon olive oil or butter
- Zest and juice of 1/2 lemon
- Salt and pepper, to taste
- Fresh parsley (optional)

Calories:	460
Protein:	27 grams
Carbohydrates:	56 grams
Fat:	14 grams
Fiber:	3 grams

Instructions:

1. Cook pasta according to package instructions
2. Heat olive oil or butter in a skillet over medium heat. Add garlic and shrimp, and cook for 2-3 minutes until shrimp are pink and opaque.
3. Add cooked linguine, lemon zest, and lemon juice, and toss to combine.
4. Season with salt and pepper, garnish with fresh parsley, and serve.

Why It's Great: This pasta is light yet flavorful, with the lemon and garlic enhancing the shrimp for a fresh, satisfying meal.

Chicken & Spinach Pasta in Tomato Cream Sauce

20 minutes

Ingredients:

- 1 cup penne or rotini pasta
- 1/2 cup cooked chicken breast (see pre-cooking instructions)
- 1/4 cup tomato sauce
- 2 tablespoons heavy cream or Greek yogurt
- 1/2 cup fresh spinach
- Salt and pepper, to taste
- Grated Parmesan (optional)

Calories:	420
Protein:	27 grams
Carbohydrates:	48 grams
Fat:	14 grams
Fiber:	4 grams

Instructions:

1. Cook pasta according to package instructions
2. Cook and slice chicken (or use pre-cooked or store bought one)
3. In a skillet over medium heat, combine tomato sauce and cream, stirring until well mixed.
4. Add cooked pasta, chicken, and spinach, and stir until heated through and spinach is wilted.
5. Season with salt and pepper, garnish with Parmesan if desired, and serve.

Why It's Great: This creamy pasta dish provides a satisfying balance of protein from the chicken, fiber from the spinach, and carbs from the pasta. The tomato cream sauce adds richness, making it a comforting meal while still supporting steady energy levels.

Quick Skillets & Casseroles

One-Pan Chicken & Veggie Skillet

20 minutes

Ingredients:

- 1/2 lb chicken breast, cubed (see pre-cooking instructions)
- 1/2 cup bell pepper, diced
- 1/2 cup zucchini, diced
- 1/2 cup cherry tomatoes, halved
- 1 tablespoon olive oil
- Salt and pepper, to taste
- Fresh basil or parsley (optional)

Calories:	320
Protein:	36 grams
Carbohydrates:	10 grams
Fat:	14 grams
Fiber:	3 grams

Instructions:

1. Heat olive oil in a large skillet over medium heat.
2. Add chicken and cook until lightly browned (if using pre-cooked chicken, just warm it up).
3. Add bell pepper, zucchini, and cherry tomatoes; season with salt and pepper.
4. Sauté for 5-7 minutes until veggies are tender and chicken is cooked through.
5. Garnish with fresh herbs if desired and serve.

Why It's Great: This skillet meal is packed with lean protein and a colorful array of vegetables, making it a nutrient-dense, low-carb option perfect for a healthy and satisfying meal. The fresh basil or parsley adds a burst of flavor without adding calories!

Beef & Rice Skillet

20 minutes - Precooked ingredients required

Ingredients:

- 1/2 lb ground beef (see pre-cooking instructions)
- 1 cup cooked brown rice (see pre-cooking instructions)
- 1/2 cup bell pepper, diced
- 1/2 cup corn kernels (canned or fresh)
- 1/2 teaspoon cumin
- Salt and pepper, to taste
- Fresh cilantro (optional)

Calories:	450
Protein:	30 grams
Carbohydrates:	38 grams
Fat:	20 grams
Fiber:	4 grams

Instructions:

1. Heat a large skillet over medium heat.
2. Cook ground beef with salt and pepper (see precooking instructions)
3. Add bell pepper, corn, and cooked brown rice.
4. Stir and cook until heated through, about 5 minutes.
5. Season with additional salt, pepper, and cumin if needed, garnish with cilantro, and serve.

Why It's Great: This skillet recipe offers a hearty mix of protein, fiber, and whole grains, making it a balanced, energy-boosting meal perfect for lunch or dinner. The cumin adds a warm, earthy flavor, and the fresh cilantro gives it a refreshing finish!

Cheesy Broccoli & Quinoa Casserole

30 minutes

Ingredients:

- 1 cup quinoa
- 1/2 cup broccoli florets
- 1/4 cup shredded cheese (cheddar or mozzarella)
- 1/4 cup Greek yogurt or sour cream
- Salt and pepper, to taste

Calories:	310
Protein:	15 grams
Carbohydrates:	34 grams
Fat:	12 grams
Fiber:	4 grams

Instructions:

1. Preheat oven to 375°F (190°C).
2. Cook quinoa and blanch broccoli (see pre-cooking instructions)
3. In a mixing bowl, combine cooked quinoa, blanched broccoli, shredded cheese, and Greek yogurt. Season with salt and pepper.
4. Transfer to a small baking dish and bake for 10-15 minutes until cheese is melted and bubbly.
5. Serve warm.

Why It's Great: This casserole is comforting, nutritious, and creamy without being overly heavy, thanks to the protein-rich quinoa and Greek yogurt.

Chicken & Spinach with Tomato Sauce

20 minutes

Ingredients:

- 1/2 lb chicken breast
- 1 cup spinach
- 1/2 cup marinara sauce
- 1 tablespoon olive oil
- Salt and pepper, to taste
- Grated Parmesan (optional)

Calories:	270
Protein:	35 grams
Carbohydrates:	7 grams
Fat:	10 grams
Fiber:	2 grams

Instructions:

1. Heat olive oil in a skillet over medium heat.
2. Add sliced chicken and cook until lightly browned.
3. Add spinach and marinara sauce, and cook for 3-4 minutes until spinach is wilted and sauce is heated through.
4. Season with salt and pepper, garnish with Parmesan if desired, and serve.

Why It's Great: This simple skillet meal is packed with protein and iron, making it a nutritious and filling option.

Mexican-Style Rice & Bean Casserole (V)

25 minutes – Precooked ingredients required

Ingredients:

- 1 cup cooked brown rice (see pre-cooking instructions)
- 1/2 cup canned black beans, rinsed and drained
- 1/4 cup corn kernels
- 1/4 cup shredded cheese (cheddar or Monterey Jack)
- 1/2 cup salsa
- Fresh cilantro (optional)

Calories:	365
Protein:	14 grams
Carbohydrates:	54 grams
Fat:	10 grams
Fiber:	8 grams

Instructions:

1. Preheat oven to 375°F (190°C).
2. In a mixing bowl, combine cooked rice, black beans, corn, shredded cheese, and salsa.
3. Transfer to a small baking dish and bake for 15-20 minutes until heated through and cheese is melted.
4. Garnish with fresh cilantro if desired and serve.

Why It's Great: This vegetarian casserole is high in protein and fiber, with Mexican-inspired flavors that make it both tasty and satisfying.

Sausage & Veggie Skillet

20 minutes

Ingredients:

- 1/2 lb sausage (chicken, turkey, or pork), sliced
- 1/2 cup bell peppers, sliced
- 1/2 cup zucchini, sliced
- 1 tablespoon olive oil
- Salt and pepper, to taste

Calories:	340
Protein:	20 grams
Carbohydrates:	9 grams
Fat:	24 grams
Fiber:	2 grams

Instructions:

1. Heat olive oil in a large skillet over medium heat.
2. Add sliced sausage and cook until browned, about 5 minutes.
3. Add bell peppers and zucchini, and cook for another 5-7 minutes until veggies are tender.
4. Season with salt and pepper, and serve.

Why It's Great: This skillet meal is filling, flavorful, and easy to make, with the sausage adding savory richness to the veggies.

Italian-Inspired Eggplant Parmesan Casserole

25 minutes

Ingredients:

- 1 small eggplant, sliced
- 1/2 cup marinara sauce
- 1/4 cup shredded mozzarella cheese
- 1 tablespoon grated Parmesan
- Salt and pepper, to taste
- Fresh basil, for garnish (optional)

Calories:	180
Protein:	10 grams
Carbohydrates:	14 grams
Fat:	10 grams
Fiber:	5 grams

Instructions:

1. Preheat oven to 375°F (190°C).
2. Arrange eggplant slices in a baking dish, and season with salt and pepper.
3. Layer marinara sauce and mozzarella cheese over the eggplant.
4. Sprinkle with grated Parmesan and bake for 20-25 minutes until eggplant is tender and cheese is melted.
5. Garnish with fresh basil if desired and serve.

Why It's Great: This lighter version of eggplant Parmesan is packed with veggies and Italian flavors, making it satisfying without being heavy.

Tuna & Rice Casserole

20 minutes - Precooked ingredients required

Ingredients:

- 1 can tuna, drained
- 1 cup cooked brown rice (see pre-cooking instructions)
- 1/4 cup Greek yogurt
- 1/4 cup shredded cheddar
- Salt and pepper, to taste
- Chopped parsley or green onions

Calories:	320
Protein:	24 grams
Carbohydrates:	30 grams
Fat:	12 grams
Fiber:	2 grams

Instructions:

1. Preheat oven to 375°F (190°C).
2. In a mixing bowl, combine tuna, cooked rice, Greek yogurt, shredded cheese, salt, and pepper.
3. Transfer the mixture to a small baking dish and bake for 15-20 minutes until the cheese is melted and the casserole is heated through.
4. Garnish with chopped parsley or green onions if desired and serve warm.

Why It's Great: This casserole is easy to make, high in protein, and creamy without being heavy, making it a nutritious and satisfying choice.

Turkey & Sweet Potato Skillet

25 minutes

Ingredients:

- 1/2 lb ground turkey
- 1 small sweet potato, diced
- 1/4 cup diced onion
- 1 clove garlic, minced
- 1 tablespoon olive oil
- Salt and pepper, to taste
- Fresh parsley (optional)

Calories:	360
Protein:	30 grams
Carbohydrates:	25 grams
Fat:	14 grams
Fiber:	4 grams

Instructions:

1. Heat olive oil in a large skillet over medium heat.
2. Add diced sweet potatoes and cook for 5-7 minutes until they begin to soften.
3. Add onion and garlic, and cook for another 2-3 minutes until fragrant.
4. Push veggies to one side, add ground turkey, and cook until browned and cooked through, about 5-7 minutes.
5. Mix everything together, season with salt and pepper, garnish with parsley if desired, and serve.

Why It's Great: This dish combines lean protein with complex carbs from the sweet potato, making it both filling and balanced.

Cheesy Cauliflower & Chicken Casserole

25 minutes

Ingredients:

- 1/2 lb chicken breast
- 1 cup cauliflower florets, blanched
- 1/4 cup shredded cheddar
- 1/4 cup Greek yogurt
- Salt and pepper, to taste
- Fresh chives (optional)

Calories:	320
Protein:	38 grams
Carbohydrates:	8 grams
Fat:	14 grams
Fiber:	2 grams

Instructions:

1. Preheat oven to 375°F (190°C).
2. Cook and shred chicken
3. Blanch cauliflower (you can use pre-cooked ingredients to speed the process)
4. In a mixing bowl, combine shredded chicken, blanched cauliflower, shredded cheese, and Greek yogurt or sour cream. Season with salt and pepper.
5. Transfer to a small baking dish and bake for 15-20 minutes until cheese is melted and casserole is heated through.
6. Garnish with fresh chives if desired and serve warm.

Why It's Great: This casserole is creamy, cheesy, and low in carbs, with cauliflower adding fiber and nutrients without heaviness.

Soups & Stews

Classic Chicken Vegetable Soup

30 minutes

Ingredients:

- 1/2 lb chicken breast
- 1/2 cup carrots, sliced
- 1/2 cup celery, sliced
- 1/2 cup diced onion
- 1 cup baby spinach
- 4 cups chicken broth
- Salt and pepper, to taste
- Fresh parsley (optional)

Calories:	220
Protein:	28 grams
Carbohydrates:	10 grams
Fat:	7 grams
Fiber:	2 grams

Instructions:

1. Cook and shred chicken.
2. In a large pot, heat a small amount of oil over medium heat. Add carrots, celery, and onion, and sauté for 5 minutes until softened.
3. Add chicken broth and bring to a boil.
4. Reduce heat to low, add shredded chicken, and simmer for 10-15 minutes.
5. Stir in baby spinach just before serving and season with salt and pepper.
6. Garnish with fresh parsley if desired and serve warm.

Why It's Great: This classic soup is light, comforting, and packed with veggies and lean protein, perfect for any time of the year.

Lentil & Vegetable Stew

30 minutes – Precooked ingredients required

Ingredients:

- 1 cup cooked lentils (see pre-cooking instructions)
- 1/2 cup carrots, diced
- 1/2 cup potatoes, diced
- 1/4 cup celery, diced
- 1/2 cup diced tomatoes (canned or fresh)
- 4 cups vegetable broth
- 1 teaspoon dried thyme
- Salt and pepper, to taste
- Fresh parsley (optional)

Calories:	230
Protein:	13 grams
Carbohydrates:	39 grams
Fat:	2 grams
Fiber:	12 grams

Instructions:

1. In a large pot, heat a small amount of oil over medium heat. Add carrots, potatoes, and celery, and sauté for 5 minutes.
2. Add vegetable broth, tomatoes, and thyme, and bring to a boil.
3. Reduce heat, add cooked lentils, and simmer for 15-20 minutes until vegetables are tender.
4. Season with salt and pepper, garnish with parsley if desired, and serve warm.

Why It's Great: This stew is filling, nutritious, and entirely plant-based, making it a great option for vegetarians and vegans.

Quick Beef & Vegetable Stew

25 minutes

Ingredients:

- 1/2 lb lean beef (such as sirloin or flank steak), diced
- 1/2 cup carrots, diced
- 1/2 cup bell peppers, diced
- 1/2 cup broccoli florets
- 1/4 cup onion, chopped
- 2 cups low-sodium beef broth
- 1 tablespoon low-sodium soy sauce
- 1 clove garlic, minced
- 1 tablespoon olive oil
- Salt and pepper, to taste
- Optional: fresh parsley

Calories:	300
Protein:	28 grams
Carbohydrates:	14 grams
Fat:	14 grams
Fiber:	3 grams

Instructions:

1. Heat olive oil in a large pot over medium heat. Add the diced beef and cook for 3-4 minutes until browned on all sides.
2. Add chopped onion and minced garlic to the pot, cooking for an additional 2 minutes until the onion is translucent.
3. Pour in the beef broth and soy sauce. Bring to a boil, then reduce the heat and let it simmer for about 10 minutes.
4. Add the carrots, bell peppers, and broccoli to the pot. Continue to simmer for another 5-7 minutes until the vegetables are tender.
5. Season with salt and pepper to taste. If desired, garnish with fresh parsley before serving.

Why It's Great: This stew is a protein-packed, nutrient-rich meal combining lean beef and vibrant vegetables in a light broth. It's perfect for a quick yet comforting and energy-sustaining lunch or dinner.

Creamy Tomato Basil Soup

25 minutes

Ingredients:

- 1 can (14.5 oz) diced tomatoes
- 1/2 cup vegetable or chicken broth
- 1/4 cup heavy cream or coconut milk for dairy-free option
- 1/4 cup diced onion
- 1 clove garlic, minced
- Fresh basil, chopped
- Salt and pepper, to taste

Calories:	132
Protein:	3 grams
Carbohydrates:	12 grams
Fat:	9 grams
Fiber:	3 grams

Instructions:

1. Heat a small amount of oil in a pot over medium heat. Add onion and garlic, and sauté for 3-4 minutes until softened.
2. Add diced tomatoes and broth, and bring to a boil.
3. Reduce heat and simmer for 10-15 minutes.
4. Use an immersion blender to blend until smooth. Stir in cream, season with salt and pepper, and garnish with basil.

Why It's Great: This soup is creamy, comforting, and full of flavor from the fresh basil, perfect for a cozy meal.

Chicken Tortilla Soup

30 minutes

Ingredients:

- 1/2 lb cooked chicken
- 1/2 cup diced tomatoes
- 1/4 cup black beans, rinsed and drained
- 1/4 cup corn kernels
- 4 cups chicken broth
- 1 teaspoon chili powder
- Salt and pepper, to taste
- Tortilla strips, for garnish
- Fresh cilantro (optional)

Calories:	186
Protein:	17 grams
Carbohydrates:	14 grams
Fat:	6 grams
Fiber:	3 grams

Instructions:

1. Cook and shred chicken
2. In a large pot, combine chicken broth, diced tomatoes, black beans, corn, and chili powder.
3. Bring to a boil, then reduce heat and add shredded chicken.
4. Simmer for 10-15 minutes, season with salt and pepper.
5. Serve topped with tortilla strips and fresh cilantro if desired.

Why It's Great: This soup is packed with flavor, protein, and fiber, making it a hearty, satisfying meal with a touch of spice.

Butternut Squash & Apple Soup

30 minutes

Ingredients:

- 1 cup butternut squash, cubed
- 1/2 apple, peeled and diced
- 1/4 cup diced onion
- 2 cups vegetable broth
- 1/4 cup coconut milk (or heavy cream for a creamier version)
- Salt and pepper, to taste

Calories:	138
Protein:	2 grams
Carbohydrates:	25 grams
Fat:	5 grams
Fiber:	4 grams

Instructions:

1. In a pot, heat a small amount of oil over medium heat. Add onion, squash, and apple, and sauté for 5 minutes until softened.
2. Add vegetable broth and bring to a boil.
3. Reduce heat and simmer for 15-20 minutes until squash is tender.
4. Use an immersion blender to blend until smooth. Stir in coconut milk, season with salt and pepper, and serve.

Why It's Great: This soup is warm, comforting, and has a unique sweet-savory flavor from the squash and apple, perfect for cooler weather.

Spicy Black Bean Soup

25 minutes

Ingredients:

- Fresh cilantro (optional)

- 1 can black beans
- 1/2 cup diced tomatoes
- 1/4 cup diced bell pepper
- 1/4 cup diced onion
- 2 cups vegetable broth
- 1 teaspoon chili powder
- Salt and pepper, to taste

Calories:	190
Protein:	9 grams
Carbohydrates:	30 grams
Fat:	3 grams
Fiber:	8 grams

Instructions:

1. In a pot, heat a small amount of oil over medium heat. Add onion and bell pepper, and sauté for 3-4 minutes until softened.
2. Add rinsed and drained black beans, diced tomatoes, vegetable broth, and chili powder. Bring to a boil then reduce heat and simmer for 10-15 minutes.
3. Use an immersion blender to blend until slightly chunky, if desired. Season with salt and pepper and garnish with cilantro.

Why It's Great: This soup is high in protein and fiber, with a satisfying spicy kick, making it a filling and nutritious meal.

Potato Leek Soup

30 minutes

Ingredients:

- 1 cup potatoes, peeled and diced
- 1/2 cup leeks, sliced and thoroughly cleaned
- 2 cups vegetable or chicken broth
- 1/4 cup heavy cream (optional for added creaminess)
- Salt and pepper, to taste
- Fresh chives (optional)

Calories:	180
Protein:	4 grams
Carbohydrates:	28 grams
Fat:	6 grams
Fiber:	3 grams

Instructions:

1. In a pot, heat a small amount of oil over medium heat. Add leeks and sauté for 5 minutes until softened.
2. Add diced potatoes and broth, and bring to a boil.
3. Reduce heat and simmer for 15-20 minutes until potatoes are tender.
4. Use an immersion blender to blend until smooth, or leave slightly chunky for more texture.
5. Stir in heavy cream if desired, and season with salt and pepper.
6. Garnish with fresh chives if desired and serve warm.

Why It's Great: This soup is creamy, mild, and comforting, with the leeks adding a gentle, onion-like flavor that pairs well with the potatoes.

Tuscan White Bean Soup

25 minutes

Ingredients:

- 1 can (15 oz) white beans
- 1/2 cup diced tomatoes
- 1/2 cup kale, chopped
- 1/4 cup diced onion
- 2 cups vegetable broth
- 1 teaspoon dried Italian herbs
- Salt and pepper, to taste
- Grated Parmesan (optional)

Calories:	190
Protein:	9 grams
Carbohydrates:	30 grams
Fat:	4 grams
Fiber:	7 grams

Instructions:

1. Heat a small amount of oil in a pot over medium heat. Add onion and sauté for 3-4 minutes until softened.
2. Add tomatoes, white beans, kale, vegetable broth, and Italian herbs.
3. Bring to a boil, then reduce heat and simmer for 10-15 minutes until kale is tender.
4. Season with salt and pepper, garnish with Parmesan if desired, and serve.

Why It's Great: This soup is rich in fiber and plant-based protein, with Italian flavors that make it warm and satisfying.

Thai Coconut Curry Soup

25 minutes

Ingredients:

- 1/2 cup sliced mushrooms
- 1/4 cup sliced bell pepper
- 1/2 cup coconut milk
- 2 cups vegetable or chicken broth
- 1 tablespoon red curry paste
- 1/4 cup shredded carrots
- Fresh cilantro (optional)
- Lime wedge (optional)

Calories:	190
Protein:	3 grams
Carbohydrates:	14 grams
Fat:	14 grams
Fiber:	3 grams

Instructions:

1. In a pot, bring broth to a simmer over medium heat. Add red curry paste and stir until dissolved.
2. Add mushrooms, bell pepper, and carrots, and cook for 5-7 minutes until vegetables are tender.
3. Stir in coconut milk and heat through.
4. Garnish with fresh cilantro and a squeeze of lime if desired, and serve warm.

Why It's Great: This soup is creamy, aromatic, and slightly spicy, with coconut milk adding richness and a hint of sweetness.

Baked & Roasted Dishes

Baked Lemon Herb Salmon with Sweet Potato Mash

30 minutes

Ingredients:

- 1/2 cup mashed sweet potato (cooked, plain)
- 1 salmon fillet (about 6 oz)
- 1 tablespoon olive oil
- Juice of 1/2 lemon
- 1/2 teaspoon dried thyme or fresh thyme leaves
- Milk for potato mash
- Salt and pepper, to taste
- Lemon slices, for garnish

Calories:	375
Protein:	33 grams
Carbohydrates:	21 grams
Fat:	18 grams
Fiber:	3 grams

Instructions:

1. Preheat oven to 400°F (200°C).
2. Peel the sweet potatoes and cut them into 1-inch cubes to ensure even cooking.
3. Bring a large pot of water to a boil. Add the sweet potato cubes and cook for 15–20 minutes or until fork-tender.
4. In the meantime place the salmon fillet on a lined baking sheet. Drizzle with olive oil and lemon juice, and sprinkle with thyme, salt, and pepper.
5. Bake for 12-15 minutes until the salmon is opaque and flakes easily with a fork.
6. Add milk to sweet potatoes. Use a potato masher or fork to mash the sweet potatoes until smooth. Adjust the texture by adding more milk if needed.
7. Serve salmon next to potato mash, garnish with lemon slices.

Why It's Great: This dish is light, flavorful, and rich in omega-3 fatty acids, making it both delicious and heart-healthy.

Roasted Vegetable Medley with Baked Chicken

30 minutes

Ingredients:

- 1 chicken breast
- 1/2 cup carrots, sliced
- 1/2 cup zucchini, sliced
- 1/2 cup bell peppers, diced
- 1/2 cup broccoli florets
- 1 tablespoon olive oil
- Salt and pepper, to taste
- Fresh rosemary (optional)

Calories:	320
Protein:	38 grams
Carbohydrates:	12 grams
Fat:	13 grams
Fiber:	4 grams

Instructions:

1. Preheat oven to 425°F (220°C).
2. In a large bowl, toss all vegetables with olive oil, salt, and pepper.
3. Season the chicken breast with salt, pepper, and any preferred spices (e.g., paprika, garlic powder, or thyme).
4. Place the seasoned chicken breast on one side of a baking sheet and spread the vegetables on the other side in a single layer.
5. Roast for 20-25 minutes until tender and slightly caramelized, stirring halfway through.
6. Garnish with fresh herbs if desired and serve warm.

Why It's Great: Roasting enhances the natural sweetness of vegetables, making them a delicious, nutrient-dense option for any meal.

Baked Chicken Parmesan with Mixed Greens Salad

30 minutes

Ingredients:

- 1 chicken breast
- 1/4 cup marinara sauce
- 1/4 cup mozzarella cheese
- 2 ts grated Parmesan cheese
- 2 cups mixed greens (e.g., spinach, arugula, and romaine)
- 1/4 cup cherry tomatoes, halved
- 1/4 cucumber, sliced
- 1 tablespoon olive oil
- 1 tablespoon balsamic vinegar or lemon juice
- Salt and pepper, to taste
- Fresh basil (optional)

Calories:	430
Protein:	39 grams
Carbohydrates:	13 grams
Fat:	26 grams
Fiber:	3 grams

Instructions:

1. Preheat the oven to 375°F (190°C).
2. Season the pounded to even thickness chicken breast with salt and pepper on both sides.
3. Place the chicken on a baking sheet lined with parchment paper or in a greased baking dish.
4. Bake for 15 minutes, then remove from the oven and spoon the marinara sauce over the top.
5. Sprinkle the shredded mozzarella and grated Parmesan cheeses evenly over the marinara sauce.
6. Return the chicken to the oven and bake for an additional 5-7 minutes, or until the cheese is melted and bubbly and the chicken reaches an internal temperature of 165°F (74°C).Garnish with fresh basil if desired and serve.
7. In a large bowl, combine the mixed greens, cherry tomatoes, and cucumber.
8. Drizzle with olive oil and balsamic vinegar (or lemon juice).
9. Toss gently to coat and season with salt and pepper to taste.
10. Serve the chicken next to it and garnish with fresh basil if desired

Why It's Great: This baked version of Chicken Parmesan is lower in fat and calories but still packed with flavor and cheesy goodness.

Stuffed Bell Peppers

30 minutes – Precooked ingredients required

Ingredients:

- 2 bell peppers, tops cut off and seeds removed
- 1/2 cup cooked ground turkey (see pre-cooking instructions)
- 1/4 cup cooked brown rice (see pre-cooking instructions)
- 1/4 cup diced tomatoes
- 1/4 cup shredded cheese (optional)
- Salt and pepper, to taste

Calories:	290
Protein:	25 grams
Carbohydrates:	18 grams
Fat:	12 grams
Fiber:	4 grams

Instructions:

1. Preheat oven to 375°F (190°C).
2. In a bowl, combine cooked ground turkey, brown rice, and diced tomatoes. Season with salt and pepper.
3. Stuff the mixture into the bell peppers and top with shredded cheese if desired.
4. Place the peppers in a baking dish and bake for 25-30 minutes until the peppers are tender.
5. Serve warm.

Why It's Great: This dish is balanced, filling, and packed with protein and fiber, making it a perfect main course.

Baked Sweet Potatoes with Black Beans and Avocado (V)

30 minutes

Ingredients:

- 1 medium sweet potato
- 1/4 cup black beans, rinsed and drained
- 1/4 avocado, diced
- Salt and pepper, to taste
- Fresh cilantro (optional)

Calories:	280
Protein:	6 grams
Carbohydrates:	45 grams
Fat:	9 grams
Fiber:	10 grams

Instructions:

1. Preheat oven to 400°F (200°C).
2. Pierce the sweet potato several times with a fork and place on a baking sheet.
3. Bake for 25-30 minutes until tender.
4. Cut the sweet potato open and top with black beans and diced avocado. Season with salt and pepper and garnish with cilantro if desired.

Why It's Great: This dish is full of fiber, healthy fats, and plant-based protein, making it both delicious and filling.

Eggplant & Tomato Bake (V)

30 minutes

Ingredients:

- 1 small eggplant
- 1/2 cup diced tomatoes
- 1/2 cup canned white beans
- 1/4 cup mozzarella cheese
- 1 tablespoon olive oil
- Salt and pepper, to taste
- Fresh basil (optional)

Calories:	345
Protein:	15 grams
Carbohydrates:	30 grams
Fat:	20 grams
Fiber:	9 grams

Instructions:

1. Preheat your oven to 375°F (190°C).
2. Brush the eggplant slices with olive oil and sprinkle with salt and pepper. Arrange them in a baking dish. Rinse and drain white beans
3. Spoon the diced tomatoes evenly over the eggplant slices. Scatter the white beans over the tomatoes.
4. Sprinkle shredded mozzarella cheese evenly over the beans and vegetables.
5. Bake in the preheated oven for 20-25 minutes, or until the cheese is melted and bubbly, and the eggplant is tender.
6. Garnish and serve: Garnish with fresh basil if desired, and serve warm.

Why It's Great: This simple bake is full of Mediterranean flavors, with tender eggplant, juicy tomatoes, and gooey cheese.

Herb-Roasted Chicken Thighs with Green Beans

30 minutes

Ingredients:

- 2 bone-in, skin-on chicken thighs
- 1/2 teaspoon dried rosemary
- 1/2 teaspoon dried thyme
- Salt and pepper, to taste
- 1 cup green beans, trimmed
- Olive oil
- 1 clove garlic, minced (optional)

Calories:	430
Protein:	28 grams
Carbohydrates:	8 grams
Fat:	32 grams
Fiber:	3 grams

Instructions:

1. Preheat your oven to 400°F (200°C).
2. Rub the chicken thighs with 1 tablespoon olive oil, dried rosemary, thyme, salt, and pepper. Place the chicken thighs on a baking sheet or in an oven-safe skillet. Roast for 25-30 minutes, or until the internal temperature reaches 165°F (74°C) and the skin is golden and crispy.
3. While the chicken is roasting, toss the green beans with 1 teaspoon olive oil, garlic (if using), salt, and pepper.
4. Add the green beans to the baking sheet with the chicken during the last 10-12 minutes of cooking. Stir them halfway through to ensure even roasting.
5. Place the chicken thighs alongside the roasted green beans. Garnish with fresh herbs like parsley or thyme, if desired.

Why It's Great: This recipe combines the savory, crispy chicken thighs with tender, flavorful green beans. It's a balanced, nutrient-dense meal, high in protein and rich in vitamins, that comes together quickly in a single pan.

Note: For a leaner option, you can remove the chicken skin before serving, which will reduce fat content significantly.

Roasted Cauliflower with Tahini Drizzle and Couscous

25 minutes

Ingredients:

- 1 small head of cauliflower
- 1 tablespoon olive oil
- Salt and pepper, to taste
- 2 tablespoons tahini
- 1 tablespoon lemon juice
- 1 tablespoon water
- 1/4 cup dry couscous

Calories:	440
Protein:	12 grams
Carbohydrates:	35 grams
Fat:	30 grams
Fiber:	5 grams

Instructions:

1. Preheat oven to 425°F (220°C).
2. Toss cauliflower florets with olive oil, salt, and pepper, and spread on a baking sheet.
3. Roast for 20-25 minutes until golden and tender.
4. In the meantime cook couscous (see pre-cooking instructions)
5. In a small bowl, whisk together tahini, lemon juice, and water until smooth.
6. Place the cooked couscous on a plate. Top with the roasted cauliflower. Drizzle the tahini sauce over the cauliflower and couscous.

Why It's Great: This dish is a tasty, nutrient-rich side, with the tahini adding healthy fats and a nutty flavor that complements the roasted cauliflower.

Baked Cod with Garlic and Herbs on Quinoa

25 minutes

Ingredients:

- 1 cod fillet (about 6 oz)
- 1/4 cup uncooked quinoa
- 1 tablespoon olive oil, divided
- 1 clove garlic, minced
- 1/2 teaspoon dried thyme
- 1/4 teaspoon salt
- Pepper, to taste
- 1/2 cup vegetable/chicken broth
- Lemon wedges, for serving
- Fresh parsley (optional)

Calories:	446
Protein:	37 grams
Carbohydrates:	35 grams
Fat:	17 grams
Fiber:	3 grams

Instructions:

1. Preheat your oven to 400°F (200°C).
2. Rinse quinoa under cold water.
3. In a small saucepan, combine the quinoa and broth. Bring to a boil, reduce heat to low, cover, and simmer for 15 minutes or until the liquid is absorbed. Fluff with a fork and set aside.
4. Place the cod fillet on a baking sheet lined with parchment paper.
5. Drizzle with 1/2 tablespoon olive oil and sprinkle with garlic, thyme, salt, and pepper.
6. Bake for 12-15 minutes, or until the fish flakes easily with a fork.
7. Place the cooked quinoa on a plate or shallow bowl. Top with the baked cod. Drizzle the remaining 1/2 tablespoon olive oil over the quinoa for added flavor. Garnish with parsley and serve with lemon wedges.

Why It's Great: This dish is flavorful, and high in protein, with fresh garlic and herbs enhancing the delicate flavor of the cod.

Garlic Parmesan Roasted Brussels Sprouts

30 minutes

Ingredients:

Calories:	446
Protein:	37 grams
Carbohydrates:	35 grams
Fat:	17 grams
Fiber:	3 grams

- 1 cup Brussels sprouts
- 1 tablespoon olive oil, divided
- 1 clove garlic, minced
- 2 tablespoons Parmesan cheese
- 1/4 block firm tofu (about 3 oz), cut into cubes
- 1/4 teaspoon salt
- Pepper, to taste
- Fresh parsley (optional)

Instructions:

1. Preheat the oven to 400°F (200°C).
2. Toss the trimmed and halved Brussels sprouts with 1/2 tablespoon olive oil, garlic, salt, and pepper.
3. Spread them on a baking sheet and roast for 20-25 minutes, stirring halfway through, until golden and tender.
4. During the last 5 minutes, sprinkle grated Parmesan cheese on top and allow it to melt.
5. While the Brussels sprouts are roasting, heat 1/2 tablespoon olive oil in a skillet over medium heat.
6. Add the tofu cubes, seasoning with a pinch of salt and pepper. Sear for 2-3 minutes per side until golden and crispy.
7. Remove from heat and set aside.
8. Plate the roasted Brussels sprouts and top with the pan-seared tofu.
9. Garnish with fresh parsley if desired and serve warm.

Why It's Great: This dish combines the hearty, roasted flavor of Brussels sprouts with the plant-based protein of tofu. The Parmesan and garlic add a delicious depth of flavor, making it a satisfying, nutrient-dense meal.

Chapter 5

Energizing Snacks

In a world that keeps us constantly moving, snacking is more than just a convenience—it's an essential part of staying fueled and focused throughout the day. While meals provide the foundation for our nutrition, snacks play a key role in bridging the gap between them, preventing energy crashes, and keeping hunger at bay. For busy people, snacks are often the quickest and most practical way to refuel without interrupting your schedule. However, what we snack on makes all the difference.

The **Good Energy Diet** emphasizes snacks that are balanced, nutritious, and easy to prepare or take on-the-go. Unlike the typical sugary or highly processed snacks that can cause energy spikes and subsequent crashes, the snacks in this section are carefully crafted to provide steady energy through a balanced combination of protein, healthy fats, and complex carbohydrates. Protein and fiber help keep you full, while healthy fats offer long-lasting energy, and complex carbs provide a steady source of fuel for your brain and body.

Why Are Energizing Snacks Important?

Throughout the day, our energy levels can fluctuate, especially between meals. When we feel tired or "hangry", it's often because our blood sugar has dropped too low. Snacks can help stabilize blood sugar, preventing those mid-morning and mid-afternoon slumps. By choosing the right snacks, we support our energy levels and improve our focus, productivity, and mood.

When Should You Snack?

While everyone's body and schedule are unique, there are a few times when snacking can be especially helpful:

- **Mid-Morning (Around 10-11 AM):** A snack between breakfast and lunch can help maintain energy levels, especially if you had an early breakfast or a long gap between meals.

- **Mid-Afternoon (Around 2-4 PM):** This is often when energy levels dip, making it a perfect time for a quick, energizing snack to keep you going until dinner.

- **Before or After Exercise:** A small, balanced snack can fuel your workout or help replenish your energy afterward.

How to Choose the Right Snack

When choosing a snack, aim for options that combine protein, healthy fats, and fiber-rich carbs. This balance will give you energy that lasts, rather than a quick spike followed by a crash. Whole foods, like fruits, vegetables, nuts, and dairy, are great choices because they're nutrient-dense and keep you satisfied longer. Avoid snacks high in refined sugars or artificial ingredients, as they can leave you feeling tired or hungry soon after.

In the following recipes, you'll find quick and easy snacks designed to fit into your busy lifestyle while helping you stay energized and focused.

Apple Slices with Almond Butter

Ingredients: 1 apple, sliced; 1 tablespoon almond butter.

Instructions: Slice the apple and spread or dip into almond butter.

Greek Yogurt with Berries

Ingredients: 1/2 cup Greek yogurt; a handful of fresh berries.

Instructions: Top Greek yogurt with berries. Optional: drizzle with honey.

Hummus & Veggie Sticks

Ingredients: 1/4 cup hummus; cucumber, carrot, and bell pepper sticks.

Instructions: Dip veggie sticks into hummus.

Cottage Cheese with Berries

Ingredients: 1/2 cup cottage cheese; a handful of fresh or frozen berries.

Instructions: Top cottage cheese with berries.

Nut & Seed Trail Mix

Ingredients: A handful of mixed nuts and seeds (almonds, walnuts, sunflower seeds).

Instructions: Mix nuts and seeds for a portable energy boost.

Hard-Boiled Egg & Cherry Tomatoes

Ingredients: 1 hard-boiled egg; a handful of cherry tomatoes.

Instructions: Enjoy as-is or sprinkle egg with a pinch of salt.

Turkey & Cheese Roll-Ups

Ingredients: 2 slices turkey breast; 1 slice cheese.

Instructions: Roll the cheese inside the turkey slices.

Simple Rice Cakes Recipe

20 minutes

Yield: About 8 small rice cakes

Ingredients:

- 1 cup cooked rice (any type: jasmine, brown, or sushi rice works well)
- 1 egg, beaten
- 2 tablespoons flour (or gluten-free flour)
- 1/4 teaspoon salt
- 1/4 teaspoon pepper (optional)
- 1 tablespoon green onion or herbs, chopped (optional, for added flavor)
- 1 tablespoon oil (for frying)

Instructions:

1. In a bowl, combine the cooked rice, beaten egg, flour, salt, and optional seasonings like pepper or green onion.
2. Mix well until the ingredients form a sticky batter that holds together.
3. Scoop a small portion (about 2 tablespoons) of the mixture and form it into a patty with your hands. Repeat until all the mixture is used.
4. Heat the oil in a non-stick skillet over medium heat.
5. Place the rice patties in the skillet, spacing them apart to avoid overcrowding.
6. Cook for 3-4 minutes per side, or until golden and crispy on the outside.
7. Transfer the rice cakes to a paper towel-lined plate to absorb excess oil.
8. Serve warm as a snack, side dish, or with a dipping sauce like soy sauce, sriracha, or a creamy dip.

Storage:

Store cooked rice cakes in an airtight container in the refrigerator for up to 3 days.

Reheat in a skillet or oven for a few minutes to restore crispiness.

Rice Cakes with Avocado

Ingredients: 1 rice cake; 1/4 avocado, mashed; salt and pepper to taste.

Instructions: Spread mashed avocado on the rice cake and season.

Almond Butter & Banana Rice Cake

Ingredients: 1 rice cake; 1 tablespoon almond butter; banana slices.

Instructions: Spread almond butter on rice cake and top with banana.

Banana & Peanut Butter

Ingredients: 1 banana; 1 tablespoon peanut butter.

Instructions: Slice banana and spread or dip with peanut butter.

Roasted Red Pepper Hummus with Pita Chips

Ingredients: 1/4 cup roasted red pepper hummus; a handful of whole-grain pita chips.

Instructions: Dip pita chips into hummus for a flavorful, protein-rich snack.

Mini Caprese Skewers

Ingredients: Cherry tomatoes; mozzarella balls; fresh basil leaves.

Instructions: Thread cherry tomato, mozzarella, and basil onto a toothpick.

Cottage Cheese & Cucumber

Ingredients: 1/2 cup cottage cheese; 1/4 cucumber, diced; salt to taste.

Instructions: Top cottage cheese with diced cucumber and sprinkle with salt.

Dark Chocolate & Almonds

Ingredients: A few squares of dark chocolate; a handful of almonds.

Instructions: Pair dark chocolate with almonds for a satisfying snack.

Greek Yogurt with Honey & Walnuts

Ingredients: 1/2 cup Greek yogurt; 1 teaspoon honey; a sprinkle of walnuts.

Instructions: Top Greek yogurt with honey and walnuts.

Baby Carrots with Ranch Greek Yogurt Dip

Ingredients: Baby carrots; 1/4 cup Greek yogurt mixed with 1/2 teaspoon ranch seasoning.

Instructions: Dip carrots in Greek yogurt ranch dip.

Apple & Cheese Slices

Ingredients: 1 apple, sliced; a few slices of cheddar cheese.

Instructions: Pair apple slices with cheese for a balanced snack.

Cucumber & Hummus Sandwich

Ingredients: Cucumber slices; 1 tablespoon hummus.

Instructions: Spread hummus between two cucumber slices.

String Cheese & Sliced Bell Pepper

Ingredients: 1 piece of string cheese; 1 bell pepper, sliced.

Instructions: Enjoy the string cheese with crisp bell pepper slices.

Mini Veggie Wrap

Ingredients: 1 small whole-grain tortilla; 1 tablespoon hummus; shredded carrots; spinach.

Instructions: Spread hummus on the tortilla, add veggies, roll up, and slice.

Fruit & Nut Bar

Ingredients:

- 1 cup mixed nuts (e.g., almonds, walnuts, cashews)
- 1 cup dried fruits (e.g., dates, apricots, raisins)
- 1/2 cup rolled oats (optional for added texture)
- 1/4 cup nut butter (e.g., almond butter, peanut butter)
- 1 tablespoon honey or maple syrup (optional for sweetness)
- 1/2 teaspoon vanilla extract (optional)
- A pinch of salt

Optional add-ins: chia seeds, flaxseeds, chocolate chips, or spices like cinnamon

Instructions:

Prepare the Ingredients:

If using whole nuts, roughly chop them to help with blending. Soak the dried fruits in warm water for about 10 minutes if they are hard or dry.

Blend the Mixture:

In a food processor, combine the nuts, dried fruits, and rolled oats (if using). Pulse until the mixture is finely chopped and well combined, but not pureed. You should still have some texture.

Add Binding Ingredients:

Add the nut butter, honey or maple syrup, vanilla extract, and salt to the mixture. Pulse again until everything is well combined. The mixture should hold together when pressed.

Shape the Bars:

Line an 8x8-inch (or similar-sized) baking dish with parchment paper, leaving some overhang for easy removal. Press the mixture firmly into the dish, spreading it evenly.

Chill:

Refrigerate the mixture for at least 1-2 hours to allow it to set.

Cut and Store:

Once firm, lift the mixture out using the parchment paper and place it on a cutting board. Cut into bars or squares as desired.
Store the bars in an airtight container in the refrigerator for up to a week or in the freezer for longer storage.

Tips:

Customize Your Bars: Feel free to experiment with different nuts, dried fruits, and add-ins to create your perfect flavor combination!
For Crunchy Bars: Lightly toast the nuts before blending for an extra depth of flavor.
Protein Boost: Add a scoop of protein powder to the mixture for a protein-packed snack.

Cottage Cheese & Crushed Walnuts

Ingredients: 1/2 cup cottage cheese; a sprinkle of crushed walnuts.

Instructions: Top cottage cheese with walnuts.

Avocado & Tuna Salad

Ingredients: Half an avocado; 2 tablespoons tuna salad.

Instructions: Fill the avocado half with tuna salad.

Whole-Grain Crackers & Cheese

Ingredients: A few whole-grain crackers; cheese slices.

Instructions: Pair crackers with cheese slices.

Protein Shake

Ingredients: 1 scoop protein powder; 1 cup almond milk.

Instructions: Blend protein powder with almond milk.

Celery Sticks with Peanut Butter

Ingredients: Celery sticks; 1 tablespoon peanut butter; a few raisins.

Instructions: Fill celery with peanut butter and top with raisins.

Edamame

Ingredients: 1/2 cup steamed edamame, sprinkled with sea salt.

Instructions: Steam and enjoy with salt.

Cottage Cheese & Peach Slices

Ingredients: 1/2 cup cottage cheese; a few slices of fresh peach.

Instructions: Top cottage cheese with peach slices.

Turkey Jerky & Almonds

Ingredients: A few slices of turkey jerky; a handful of almonds.

Instructions: Enjoy as-is.

Sliced Bell Pepper with Guacamole

Ingredients: Sliced bell pepper; 2 tablespoons guacamole.

Instructions: Dip bell pepper in guacamole.

Applesauce with Cinnamon & Almonds

Ingredients: 1/2 cup unsweetened applesauce; 1 tablespoon sliced almonds; a pinch of cinnamon.

Instructions: Sprinkle cinnamon and almonds over applesauce.

Cottage Cheese & Chopped Green Apple

Ingredients: 1/2 cup cottage cheese; green apple chunks.

Instructions: Top cottage cheese with apple.

Oatmeal Muffin

Ingredients:

- 1 1/2 cups rolled oats
- 1 cup milk (or any non-dairy milk)
- 1/4 cup honey or maple syrup
- 1/4 cup unsweetened applesauce
- 1/4 cup vegetable oil or melted coconut oil
- 1 teaspoon vanilla extract
- 1 teaspoon baking powder
- 1/2 teaspoon baking soda
- 1/2 teaspoon salt
- 1 teaspoon cinnamon (optional)
- Optional add-ins: 1/2 cup raisins, chopped nuts, or chocolate chips

Instructions:

1. Preheat the Oven: Preheat your oven to 350°F (175°C) and line a muffin tin with paper liners or lightly grease it.
2. Combine Wet Ingredients: In a large mixing bowl, combine the rolled oats and milk. Let it sit for about 10 minutes to allow the oats to soak and soften. Then, add honey or maple syrup, applesauce, vegetable oil, and vanilla extract. Mix well.
3. Mix Dry Ingredients: In another bowl, whisk together the baking powder, baking soda, salt, and cinnamon (if using).
4. Combine Mixtures: Add the dry ingredients to the wet ingredients and stir until just combined. Be careful not to overmix. If you're adding any optional ingredients like raisins, nuts, or chocolate chips, fold them in gently.
5. Fill Muffin Tins: Divide the batter evenly among the muffin cups, filling each about 3/4 full.
6. Bake: Bake in the preheated oven for 18-20 minutes, or until the muffins are golden brown and a toothpick inserted into the center comes out clean.
7. Cool: Allow the muffins to cool in the pan for 5 minutes, then transfer them to a wire rack to cool completely.

Storage:

Store cooled muffins in an airtight container at room temperature for up to 3 days or in the refrigerator for up to a week. You can also freeze them for up to 3 months. Just thaw and reheat as needed.

Greek Yogurt Parfait

Ingredients: Greek yogurt; granola; berries.

Instructions: Layer Greek yogurt, granola, and berries in a jar.

Mozzarella & Tomato Bites

Ingredients: Cherry tomatoes; mozzarella balls; balsamic glaze.

Instructions: Top tomatoes with mozzarella and drizzle with balsamic glaze.

Homemade Granola Bar

Ingredients: 2 cups oats; 1/2 cup honey; 1/2 cup nut butter; optional: nuts, dried fruits.

Instructions: Mix ingredients, press into a lined dish, and refrigerate for 1 hour. Cut into bars.

Apple with Pumpkin Seeds

Ingredients: Apple slices; 1 tablespoon pumpkin seeds.

Instructions: Pair apple slices with pumpkin seeds.

Veggie & Cheese Plate

Ingredients: A few pieces of sliced cheese with bell pepper and cucumber slices.

Instructions: Arrange on a plate and enjoy.

Turkey & Avocado Lettuce Wrap

Ingredients: A lettuce leaf wrapped around turkey and avocado slices.

Instructions: Wrap and enjoy as a light snack.

Almond Butter & Carrot Sticks

Ingredients: Carrot sticks dipped in almond butter.

Instructions: Dip and enjoy for a crunchy, sweet snack.

Protein-Packed Smoothie

Ingredients: Greek yogurt; almond milk; spinach; banana.

Instructions: Blend until smooth.

Roasted Almonds & Grapes

Ingredients: A handful of roasted almonds; a handful of grapes.

Instructions: Pair almonds with grapes for a sweet and savory snack that provides a balance of protein, healthy fats, and natural sugars.

Mini Tuna Salad Wrap

Ingredients: 1 small whole-grain tortilla; 2 tablespoons tuna salad.

Instructions: Spread the tuna salad on the tortilla, roll it up, and slice into bite-sized pieces.

Pear Slices with Ricotta Cheese

Ingredients: Pear slices; 2 tablespoons ricotta cheese.

Instructions: Spread a little ricotta cheese on each pear slice for a naturally sweet and creamy snack.

Cottage Cheese with Sunflower Seeds

Ingredients: 1/2 cup cottage cheese; 1 tablespoon sunflower seeds.

Instructions: Top cottage cheese with sunflower seeds for added crunch and healthy fats.

Hard-Boiled Egg & Spinach

Ingredients: 1 hard-boiled egg; a handful of fresh spinach or arugula.

Instructions: Pair the egg with fresh greens for a simple and nutrient-packed snack.

Stuffed Mini Bell Peppers with Feta

Ingredients: 3-4 mini bell peppers; 2 tablespoons crumbled feta cheese.

Instructions: Slice mini bell peppers in half and remove seeds. Fill each half with a small amount of feta cheese for a crunchy, savory snack.

Chapter 6

Dinner to Restore and Recharge

Dinner is a key meal in the **Good Energy Diet**—it's not just about satisfying hunger but about setting yourself up for a restful night and a strong start the next day. The right dinner can help you recharge without overloading your digestive system, ensuring that your body can focus on recovery while you sleep rather than processing heavy foods. For busy professionals, working parents, or anyone with a full schedule, a balanced, nourishing dinner plays a crucial role in maintaining steady energy levels throughout the week.

Why Dinner Matters for Energy and Recovery

When you choose your evening meal thoughtfully, you're giving your body the nutrients it needs to repair and restore. High-quality protein supports muscle recovery, while fiber-rich vegetables aid digestion and contribute to a feeling of lightness. Unlike quick energy sources that might be useful earlier in the day, a good energy dinner focuses on long-lasting nutrients that allow your body to wind down and prepare for rest.

Eating foods that are easy to digest and low in stimulants helps maintain balanced blood sugar levels, which in turn supports more restful sleep. This avoids the spikes and crashes that can disrupt sleep and leave you feeling sluggish the next day.

When to Eat Dinner for Optimal Energy

For most people, an ideal dinner time is about 2-3 hours before bed. This allows for digestion without discomfort, giving your body the chance to settle before sleep. Eating too close to bedtime can make it harder to fall asleep comfortably, while eating too early might lead to late-night hunger. Aim to have dinner around 6:30-7:30 p.m. if you plan to go to bed by 10:00 p.m., but listen to your body and schedule accordingly.

By making dinner an intentional, balanced meal, you're not only giving yourself a good energy boost for the next day but also promoting a restorative sleep cycle. Enjoy these recipes knowing they're designed to help you unwind, recharge, and maintain steady energy for whatever tomorrow brings.

Lean Proteins with Veggies

Lemon Herb Lamb Chops with Steamed Broccoli

20 minutes

Ingredients:

- 2 lamb chops
- 1/2 cup broccoli florets
- Juice of 1/4 lemon
- 1/2 tablespoon olive oil
- 1/2 teaspoon dried oregano
- 1/2 teaspoon garlic powder
- Salt and pepper, to taste
- Fresh parsley (optional)

Calories:	320
Protein:	25 grams
Carbohydrates:	6 grams
Fat:	23 grams
Fiber:	2 grams

Instructions:

1. In a bowl, mix lemon juice, olive oil, oregano, garlic powder, salt, and pepper. Toss the lamb chops in the marinade and let them sit for about 10 minutes.
2. Steam the broccoli for about 5 minutes until tender.
3. Heat a pan over medium-high heat and cook the marinated lamb chops for 3-4 minutes per side until they reach your desired level of doneness.
4. Serve the lamb chops with steamed broccoli and garnish with fresh parsley.

Why It's Great: This quick, flavorful meal combines tender lamb chops with nutrient-rich broccoli, providing a satisfying dinner that's both delicious and healthy.

Turkey Lettuce Wraps with Shredded Carrots

15 minutes

Ingredients:

- 1/2 lb ground turkey
- 1 tablespoon soy sauce
- 1/2 teaspoon garlic powder
- Salt and pepper, to taste
- Lettuce leaves (e.g., romaine or butter lettuce)
- 1/4 cup shredded carrots
- Sliced green onions, for garnish

Calories:	240
Protein:	30 grams
Carbohydrates:	6 grams
Fat:	12 grams
Fiber:	2 grams

Instructions:

1. In a skillet over medium heat, cook the ground turkey until browned, about 5-7 minutes. Add soy sauce, garlic powder, salt, and pepper to taste.
2. Spoon the turkey mixture into lettuce leaves.
3. Top with shredded carrots and sliced green onions for garnish.

Why It's Great: These wraps are low in carbs, high in protein, and perfect for a quick, refreshing meal.

Grilled Chicken with Spinach and Cherry Tomato Salad

20 minutes

Ingredients:

- 1 chicken breast, pounded to even thickness
- Salt and pepper, to taste
- 1 cup spinach
- 1/2 cup cherry tomatoes, halved
- 1 tablespoon balsamic vinegar
- 1 tablespoon olive oil

Calories:	280
Protein:	33 grams
Carbohydrates:	5 grams
Fat:	14 grams
Fiber:	2 grams

Instructions:

1. Season the chicken with salt and pepper. Grill over medium heat for 5-6 minutes per side until fully cooked.
2. In a bowl, toss spinach and cherry tomatoes with balsamic vinegar and olive oil.
3. Serve the grilled chicken alongside the salad.

Why It's Great: This meal is rich in protein, vitamins, and antioxidants, making it both nourishing and delicious.

Turkey and Zucchini Meatballs with Marinara Sauce

25 minutes

Ingredients:

- 1/2 lb ground turkey
- 1/4 cup grated zucchini
- 1/4 cup breadcrumbs (optional)
- 1/2 teaspoon garlic powder
- Salt and pepper, to taste
- 1/2 cup marinara sauce

Calories:	210
Protein:	25 grams
Carbohydrates:	8 grams
Fat:	9 grams
Fiber:	2 grams

Instructions:

1. In a bowl, mix ground turkey, grated zucchini, breadcrumbs, garlic powder, salt, and pepper.
2. Form into small meatballs.
3. Heat a skillet over medium heat, and cook the meatballs for about 5-7 minutes until browned.
4. Add marinara sauce, cover, and simmer for 5 more minutes.

Why It's Great: These meatballs are packed with lean protein and veggies, perfect for a balanced dinner.

Sautéed Beef with Bell Peppers and Snap Peas

20 minutes

Ingredients:

- 1/2 lb beef strips (sirloin or flank steak)
- 1/2 bell pepper, sliced
- 1/2 cup snap peas
- 1 tablespoon soy sauce
- 1 teaspoon sesame oil

Calories:	290
Protein:	28 grams
Carbohydrates:	8 grams
Fat:	17 grams
Fiber:	2 grams

Instructions:

1. Heat sesame oil in a pan over medium-high heat. Add beef strips and cook for 3-4 minutes until browned.
2. Add bell pepper and snap peas, and stir-fry for another 3-5 minutes until veggies are tender-crisp.
3. Drizzle with soy sauce before serving.

Why It's Great: This dish provides lean protein, healthy fats, and fiber, with plenty of flavor and color.

Garlic Rosemary Pork Chops with Green Beans

20 minutes

Ingredients:

- 2 boneless pork chops
- Salt, pepper, and garlic powder, to taste
- 1/2 teaspoon dried rosemary or fresh sprigs
- 1 cup green beans, trimmed

Calories:	320
Protein:	30 grams
Carbohydrates:	6 grams
Fat:	20 grams
Fiber:	2 grams

Instructions:

1. Season the pork chops with salt, pepper, garlic powder, and rosemary.
2. In a skillet, cook pork chops over medium heat for 5-7 minutes per side until browned and cooked through.
3. Steam or sauté the green beans while the pork chops cook.
4. Serve pork chops with green beans on the side.

Why It's Great: This meal is balanced with protein and fiber, and the flavors are rich and satisfying.

Greek Chicken with Cucumber and Feta Salad

20 minutes

Ingredients:

- 1 chicken breast, seasoned with salt, pepper, and dried oregano
- 1/2 cucumber, diced
- 1/4 cup crumbled feta cheese
- 1/4 cup cherry tomatoes, halved
- 1 tablespoon olive oil
- 1 teaspoon lemon juice

Calories:	360
Protein:	38 grams
Carbohydrates:	6 grams
Fat:	20 grams
Fiber:	1 grams

Instructions:

1. Grill or pan-sear the chicken breast over medium heat for 5-6 minutes per side until fully cooked.
2. In a bowl, combine cucumber, feta, cherry tomatoes, olive oil, and lemon juice.
3. Serve the chicken with the salad on the side.

Why It's Great: This meal offers a taste of the Mediterranean with lean protein, fresh veggies, and healthy fats.

Lemon Garlic Turkey Cutlets with Roasted Peppers

25 minutes

Ingredients:

- 2 turkey cutlets
- Juice of 1/2 lemon
- 1 clove garlic, minced
- 1 tablespoon olive oil
- Salt and pepper, to taste
- 1/2 red bell pepper, sliced

Calories:	270
Protein:	30 grams
Carbohydrates:	4 grams
Fat:	15 grams
Fiber:	1 grams

Instructions:

1. In a small bowl, mix lemon juice, garlic, olive oil, salt, and pepper.
2. Marinate the turkey cutlets in the mixture for a few minutes.
3. Heat a pan over medium heat, cook the turkey cutlets for 4-5 minutes per side until fully cooked.
4. In the same pan, sauté the bell pepper slices until tender.

Why It's Great: This dish is high in protein and bursting with flavor, thanks to the lemon-garlic marinade and roasted peppers.

Pork Tenderloin with Sautéed Spinach

20 minutes

Ingredients:

- 1 pork tenderloin, sliced into medallions
- Salt and pepper, to taste
- 1 cup spinach
- 1 tablespoon olive oil

Calories:	240
Protein:	28 grams
Carbohydrates:	2 grams
Fat:	14 grams
Fiber:	1 grams

Instructions:

1. Season the pork medallions with salt and pepper.
2. Heat olive oil in a skillet over medium-high heat and cook the pork for about 3-4 minutes per side until golden and cooked through.
3. Remove the pork and add spinach to the same pan, sautéing until wilted.

Why It's Great: This dish provides a lean source of protein and is rich in iron from the spinach, ideal for a light, nourishing meal.

Sautéed Veal with Kale and Butternut Squash

25 minutes

Ingredients:

- 1 lb veal, thinly sliced
- 2 cups butternut squash, peeled and cubed
- 2 cups kale, stems removed and chopped
- 2 tablespoons olive oil
- 2 cloves garlic, minced
- Salt and pepper, to taste
- 1 teaspoon dried thyme (optional)
- Fresh lemon juice (optional)

Calories:	360
Protein:	32 grams
Carbohydrates:	14 grams
Fat:	20 grams
Fiber:	3 grams

Instructions:

1. In a large skillet, heat 1 tablespoon of olive oil over medium heat. Add the cubed butternut squash and sauté for about 5-7 minutes until tender and slightly caramelized.
2. Push the butternut squash to the side of the skillet, add the remaining tablespoon of olive oil, and then add the thinly sliced veal. Season with salt, pepper, and thyme (if using). Cook for 3-4 minutes until the veal is browned and cooked through, stirring occasionally.
3. Add the minced garlic and chopped kale to the skillet. Stir everything together and cook for an additional 3-4 minutes until the kale is wilted and tender.
4. Adjust seasoning as needed and drizzle with fresh lemon juice before serving, if desired.

Why It's Great: This hearty meal is packed with protein from the veal, fiber from the kale, and vitamins from the butternut squash, making it a nutritious choice that's quick to prepare and full of flavor.

123

Balsamic Glazed Steak with Roasted Zucchini

25 minutes

Ingredients:

- 1/2 lb steak (such as sirloin or flank)
- Salt and pepper, to taste
- 1 tablespoon balsamic vinegar
- 1 small zucchini, sliced into rounds
- 1 tablespoon olive oil

Calories:	410
Protein:	35 grams
Carbohydrates:	6 grams
Fat:	28 grams
Fiber:	2 grams

Instructions:

1. Season the steak with salt and pepper. Sear in a hot skillet for about 3-4 minutes per side, depending on thickness and preferred doneness.
2. Drizzle with balsamic vinegar during the last minute of cooking.
3. Meanwhile, toss zucchini rounds in olive oil, salt, and pepper, and roast at 400°F (200°C) for about 15 minutes until tender.
4. Serve the steak with the roasted zucchini on the side.

Why It's Great: This meal is hearty but light, with lean steak and fiber-rich zucchini that offer a balanced dinner without feeling too heavy.

Chicken Stir-Fry with Bok Choy and Carrots

20 minutes

Ingredients:

- 1 chicken breast, sliced thinly
- 1 cup bok choy, chopped
- 1/2 cup carrots, sliced into thin rounds
- 1 tablespoon soy sauce
- 1/2 teaspoon sesame oil

Calories:	250
Protein:	30 grams
Carbohydrates:	8 grams
Fat:	10 grams
Fiber:	2 grams

Instructions:

1. In a skillet, heat sesame oil over medium-high heat. Add the chicken and cook until browned, about 5-6 minutes.
2. Add the carrots and bok choy, stirring for another 3-5 minutes until vegetables are tender-crisp.
3. Drizzle with soy sauce and serve.

Why It's Great: This dish provides lean protein, vitamins, and minerals from the bok choy and carrots, making it a balanced, flavorful meal.

Seafood Dinners

Lemon Garlic Shrimp with Zoodles

20 minutes

Ingredients:

- 1/2 lb shrimp, peeled and deveined
- 1 medium zucchini, spiralized
- 1 tablespoon olive oil
- 1 clove garlic, minced
- Juice of 1/2 lemon
- Salt and pepper, to taste

- Fresh parsley (optional)

Calories:	220
Protein:	30 grams
Carbohydrates:	6 grams
Fat:	9 grams
Fiber:	2 grams

Instructions:

1. Heat olive oil in a skillet over medium heat. Add garlic and cook for 1 minute until fragrant.
2. Add shrimp and cook for 3-4 minutes until pink and cooked through.
3. Squeeze lemon juice over shrimp and season with salt and pepper.
4. Add spiralized zucchini to the skillet and toss with the shrimp for 1-2 minutes until slightly tender.
5. Garnish with fresh parsley.

Why It's Great: This dish is high in protein and low in carbs, offering a light but satisfying dinner with a burst of flavor from the lemon and garlic.

Baked Lemon Herb Salmon with Asparagus

20 minutes

Ingredients:

- 1 salmon fillet
- 1/2 lemon, sliced
- 1/2 teaspoon dried thyme
- 1/2 teaspoon dried rosemary
- Salt and pepper, to taste
- 1 cup asparagus, trimmed

Calories:	220
Protein:	30 grams
Carbohydrates:	6 grams
Fat:	9 grams
Fiber:	2 grams

Instructions:

1. Preheat oven to 400°F (200°C).
2. Place salmon and asparagus on a baking sheet. Season with salt, pepper, thyme, and rosemary.
3. Arrange lemon slices on top of the salmon.
4. Bake for 12-15 minutes until the salmon is cooked through and asparagus is tender.

Why It's Great: This one-pan dish is simple and flavorful, combining healthy fats from the salmon with fiber-rich asparagus.

Cod with Cherry Tomatoes and Fresh Basil

20 minutes

Ingredients:

- 1 cod fillet
- 1/2 cup cherry tomatoes, halved
- 1 tablespoon olive oil
- Salt and pepper, to taste
- Fresh basil, chopped, for garnish

Calories:	250
Protein:	30 grams
Carbohydrates:	5 grams
Fat:	13 grams
Fiber:	3 grams

Instructions:

1. Heat olive oil in a skillet over medium heat. Add cherry tomatoes and cook for 3-4 minutes until softened.
2. Season cod with salt and pepper and add to the skillet.
3. Cook for 5-7 minutes per side until the cod is flaky and cooked through.
4. Garnish with fresh basil.

Why It's Great: This dish is low in calories and packed with antioxidants from the tomatoes, making it both nutritious and refreshing.

Shrimp and Mango Salad with Lime

20 minutes

Ingredients:

- 1/2 lb shrimp, peeled and deveined
- 1/2 mango, diced
- Mixed greens (e.g., spinach, arugula)
- Juice of 1 lime
- 1 tablespoon olive oil
- Salt and pepper, to taste

Calories:	260
Protein:	26 grams
Carbohydrates:	15 grams
Fat:	11 grams
Fiber:	3 grams

Instructions:

1. Sauté shrimp in a skillet over medium heat with olive oil for 3-4 minutes until pink and cooked through.
2. In a bowl, combine mixed greens, mango, and cooked shrimp.
3. Drizzle with lime juice, season with salt and pepper, and toss to combine.

Why It's Great: This salad is high in protein, with a touch of sweetness from the mango and a zesty kick from the lime.

Grilled Mahi-Mahi with Pineapple Salsa

20 minutes

Ingredients:

- 1 mahi-mahi fillet
- Salt and pepper, to taste
- 1/4 cup diced pineapple
- 1 tablespoon diced red onion
- 1 tablespoon chopped cilantro
- Juice of 1/2 lime

Calories:	230
Protein:	32 grams
Carbohydrates:	8 grams
Fat:	6 grams
Fiber:	1 grams

Instructions:

1. Season mahi-mahi with salt and pepper. Grill over medium-high heat for about 4-5 minutes per side until cooked through.
2. In a bowl, mix pineapple, red onion, cilantro, and lime juice to make the salsa.
3. Serve the grilled mahi-mahi topped with pineapple salsa.

Why It's Great: This dish is light, refreshing, and packed with flavor, perfect for a quick, healthy dinner.

Sophie Marigold

Garlic Butter Shrimp with Green Beans

20 minutes

Ingredients:

- 1/2 lb shrimp, peeled and deveined
- 1 cup green beans, trimmed
- 1 tablespoon butter
- 1 clove garlic, minced
- Salt and pepper, to taste

Calories:	220
Protein:	28 grams
Carbohydrates:	6 grams
Fat:	10 grams
Fiber:	2 grams

Instructions:

1. Melt butter in a skillet over medium heat. Add garlic and cook for 1 minute until fragrant.
2. Add shrimp and cook for 3-4 minutes until pink and cooked through. Remove shrimp from the skillet.
3. Add green beans to the skillet, season with salt and pepper, and sauté for 4-5 minutes until tender.
4. Return shrimp to the skillet and toss with green beans before serving.

Why It's Great: This dish combines lean protein and fiber-rich green beans with the indulgent flavor of garlic butter.

Tilapia with Roasted Brussels Sprouts

20 minutes

Ingredients:

- 1 tilapia fillet
- Salt and pepper, to taste
- 1 tablespoon olive oil
- 1 cup Brussels sprouts, trimmed and halved

Calories:	240
Protein:	28 grams
Carbohydrates:	8 grams
Fat:	12 grams
Fiber:	4 grams

Instructions:

1. Preheat oven to 400°F (200°C). Toss Brussels sprouts in olive oil, salt, and pepper. Roast for 15-20 minutes until crispy and golden.
2. Season tilapia with salt and pepper. Pan-sear over medium heat for 3-4 minutes per side until flaky.
3. Serve tilapia with roasted Brussels sprouts.

Why It's Great: This meal is lean and satisfying, with a great balance of protein, fiber, and healthy fats from the olive oil.

Miso Glazed Salmon with Steamed Bok Choy

20 minutes

Ingredients:

- 1 salmon fillet
- 1 tablespoon miso paste
- 1 teaspoon honey
- 1 teaspoon soy sauce
- 1 cup bok choy, chopped
- 1 tablespoon water

Calories:	290
Protein:	26 grams
Carbohydrates:	9 grams
Fat:	17 grams
Fiber:	2 grams

Instructions:

1. In a small bowl, mix miso paste, honey, and soy sauce. Brush over the salmon fillet.
2. Steam bok choy with 1 tablespoon of water in a covered skillet over medium heat for about 3-4 minutes until tender.
3. Meanwhile, cook the salmon in a skillet over medium heat for 4-5 minutes per side, or until cooked through.
4. Serve the salmon with steamed bok choy on the side.

Why It's Great: This dish is packed with healthy fats, fiber, and a satisfying umami flavor, supporting a balanced and nourishing dinner.

Lemon Dill Baked Cod with Baby Potatoes

25 minutes

Ingredients:

- 1 cod fillet
- 1/2 cup baby potatoes, halved
- 1 tablespoon olive oil
- Salt and pepper, to taste
- 1 teaspoon fresh dill, chopped
- Juice of 1/2 lemon

Calories:	280
Protein:	25 grams
Carbohydrates:	18 grams
Fat:	12 grams
Fiber:	2 grams

Instructions:

1. Preheat oven to 400°F (200°C). Toss baby potatoes with olive oil, salt, and pepper, and roast for 20-25 minutes until tender.
2. Season cod with salt, pepper, dill, and lemon juice. Place on a baking sheet and bake for 10-12 minutes until flaky.
3. Serve cod with roasted baby potatoes.

Why It's Great: This dish combines protein, healthy carbs, and fiber, while dill and lemon add a refreshing flavor.

Seared Scallops with Garlic and Lemon

20 minutes

Ingredients:

- 1/2 lb scallops
- 1 tablespoon butter
- 1 clove garlic, minced
- Juice of 1/2 lemon
- Salt and pepper, to taste
- Fresh parsley, for garnish

Calories:	280
Protein:	23 grams
Carbohydrates:	4 grams
Fat:	18 grams
Fiber:	0 grams

Instructions:

1. Pat scallops dry and season with salt and pepper.
2. Melt butter in a skillet over medium-high heat. Add scallops and sear for 2-3 minutes per side until golden.
3. Add garlic and lemon juice to the skillet and cook for 1 more minute.
4. Garnish with fresh parsley before serving.

Why It's Great: This dish is rich in lean protein, with a satisfying blend of garlic, lemon, and butter flavors.

Grilled Shrimp and Pineapple Skewers

20 minutes

Ingredients:

- 1/2 lb shrimp, peeled and deveined
- 1/2 cup fresh pineapple chunks
- Salt and pepper, to taste
- 1 tablespoon olive oil
- Wooden skewers, soaked in water

Calories:	230
Protein:	28 grams
Carbohydrates:	10 grams
Fat:	9 grams
Fiber:	1 grams

Instructions:

1. Thread shrimp and pineapple chunks onto skewers.
2. Brush with olive oil, and season with salt and pepper.
3. Grill over medium heat for about 3-4 minutes per side until shrimp is cooked through.
4. Serve with a side salad, if desired.

Why It's Great: This dish combines protein and natural sweetness from pineapple, making it light, tasty, and quick to prepare.

Blackened Catfish with Cabbage Slaw

25 minutes

Ingredients:

- 1 catfish fillet
- 1/2 teaspoon paprika
- 1/4 teaspoon cayenne pepper
- Salt and pepper, to taste
- 1 tablespoon olive oil
- 1/2 cup shredded cabbage
- 1 tablespoon Greek yogurt
- 1 teaspoon apple cider vinegar

Calories:	290
Protein:	27 grams
Carbohydrates:	6 grams
Fat:	17 grams
Fiber:	2 grams

Instructions:

1. Season catfish with paprika, cayenne pepper, salt, and pepper.
2. Heat olive oil in a skillet over medium-high heat and cook catfish for 3-4 minutes per side until blackened and flaky.
3. In a bowl, mix cabbage with Greek yogurt and apple cider vinegar to make the slaw.
4. Serve blackened catfish with cabbage slaw on the side.

Why It's Great: This meal offers a balance of lean protein, healthy fats, and fiber, with a flavorful spicy kick.

Plant-Based Meals

Quinoa and Black Bean Stuffed Bell Peppers

25 minutes – Precooked ingredients required

Ingredients:

- 2 bell peppers, halved and seeded
- 1/2 cup cooked quinoa (see pre-cooking instructions)
- 1/2 cup black beans, rinsed and drained
- 1/4 cup corn kernels
- 1/4 cup diced tomatoes
- 1/2 teaspoon cumin
- Salt and pepper, to taste

Calories:	235
Protein:	9 grams
Carbohydrates:	40 grams
Fat:	5 grams
Fiber:	9 grams

Instructions:

1. Preheat oven to 375°F (190°C).
2. In a bowl, combine cooked quinoa, black beans, corn, diced tomatoes, cumin, salt, and pepper.
3. Stuff the bell pepper halves with the mixture and place them on a baking sheet.
4. Bake for 15-20 minutes until the peppers are tender.

Why It's Great: This meal is fiber-rich and provides plant-based protein, making it filling and nutritious.

Cauliflower Fried Rice with Scrambled Eggs

15 minutes

Ingredients:

- 1 cup cauliflower rice
- 1/4 cup peas
- 1/4 cup diced carrots
- 1/4 cup diced bell pepper
- 1 tablespoon soy sauce
- 1/2 teaspoon sesame oil
- 2 eggs, lightly beaten
- Salt and pepper, to taste

Calories:	190
Protein:	11 grams
Carbohydrates:	14 grams
Fat:	10 grams
Fiber:	3 grams

Instructions:

1. Heat a non-stick skillet over medium heat and add a small amount of sesame oil or cooking spray. Pour the beaten eggs into the skillet and scramble them gently until fully cooked. Remove from the skillet and set aside.
2. In the same skillet, heat the sesame oil over medium-high heat. Add the peas, carrots, and bell peppers, and sauté for 3-4 minutes until they begin to soften.
3. Stir in the cauliflower rice and cook for another 3-4 minutes until the rice is tender and slightly golden.
4. Return the scrambled eggs to the skillet and mix with the vegetables. Add the soy sauce and stir everything until evenly combined. Season with salt and pepper to taste.
5. Transfer to a plate or bowl and serve warm. Optionally, garnish with green onions or sesame seeds for extra flavor.

Why It's Great: This dish is low in carbs and high in nutrients, providing a flavorful, light alternative to traditional fried rice.

Chickpea and Spinach Stir-Fry

15 minutes

Ingredients:

- 1 cup canned chickpeas, rinsed and drained
- 1 cup fresh spinach
- 1 tablespoon olive oil
- 1/2 teaspoon garlic powder
- Salt and pepper, to taste

Calories:	290
Protein:	11 grams
Carbohydrates:	28 grams
Fat:	14 grams
Fiber:	8 grams

Instructions:

1. Heat olive oil in a skillet over medium heat. Add chickpeas and garlic powder, and cook for 3-4 minutes.
2. Add spinach and cook until wilted, about 2-3 minutes.
3. Season with salt and pepper before serving.

Why It's Great: This simple dish is full of fiber, plant-based protein, and iron, making it nourishing and quick.

Lentil and Vegetable Stew

25 minutes

Ingredients:

- 1/2 cup lentils, rinsed
- 1/2 cup diced carrots
- 1/2 cup diced celery
- 1/2 cup diced potatoes
- 2 cups vegetable broth
- Salt and pepper, to taste

Calories:	230
Protein:	12 grams
Carbohydrates:	38 grams
Fat:	2 grams
Fiber:	12 grams

Instructions:

1. In a pot, combine lentils, carrots, celery, potatoes, and vegetable broth.
2. Bring to a boil, then reduce heat and simmer for 20-25 minutes until lentils and vegetables are tender.
3. Season with salt and pepper before serving.

Why It's Great: This stew is rich in fiber and plant-based protein, making it a filling and nourishing option.

Eggplant and Tomato Bake with Parmesan

25 minutes

Ingredients:

- 1 small eggplant, sliced
- 1/2 cup cherry tomatoes, halved
- 1 tablespoon olive oil
- Salt and pepper, to taste
- 1/4 cup grated Parmesan cheese

Calories:	180
Protein:	6 grams
Carbohydrates:	11 grams
Fat:	13 grams
Fiber:	4 grams

Instructions:

1. Preheat oven to 400°F (200°C).
2. Arrange eggplant slices and cherry tomatoes on a baking sheet. Drizzle with olive oil, and season with salt and pepper.
3. Sprinkle with Parmesan cheese and bake for 15-20 minutes until eggplant is tender.

Why It's Great: This dish is simple, delicious, and provides a good source of fiber and antioxidants from the eggplant and tomatoes.

Note: you can complete this dish with chicken or fish for more substantial meal

---

Sweet Potato and Black Bean Skillet

20 minutes

Ingredients:

- 1 small sweet potato, diced
- 1/2 cup black beans, rinsed and drained
- 1/4 cup corn kernels
- 1/2 teaspoon cumin
- Salt and pepper, to taste
- 1 tablespoon olive oil

Calories:	290
Protein:	7 grams
Carbohydrates:	44 grams
Fat:	9 grams
Fiber:	8 grams

Instructions:

1. Heat olive oil in a skillet over medium heat. Add sweet potato and cook for 8-10 minutes until tender.
2. Stir in black beans, corn, cumin, salt, and pepper, and cook for an additional 5 minutes.

Why It's Great: This meal is filling, nutritious, and packed with plant-based protein and fiber.

Sweet Potato and Brussels Sprouts Hash

25 minutes

Ingredients:

- 1/2 cup Brussels sprouts, trimmed and halved
- 1 small sweet potato, diced
- 1 tablespoon olive oil
- Salt and pepper, to taste

Calories:	210
Protein:	3 grams
Carbohydrates:	27 grams
Fat:	10 grams
Fiber:	5 grams

Instructions:

1. Heat olive oil in a skillet over medium heat. Add sweet potato and cook for 5-7 minutes until beginning to soften.
2. Add Brussels sprouts, salt, and pepper, and cook for an additional 10-12 minutes until vegetables are tender and golden.

Why It's Great: This hash is high in fiber, vitamins, and minerals, making it a wholesome plant-based dinner.

Mushroom and Spinach Sauté over Rice

20 minutes – Precooked ingredients required

Ingredients:

- 1/2 cup cooked brown or jasmine rice (see pre-cooking instructions)
- 1 cup mushrooms, sliced
- 1 cup spinach
- 1 tablespoon olive oil
- Salt and pepper, to taste

Calories:	225
Protein:	6 grams
Carbohydrates:	31 grams
Fat:	9 grams
Fiber:	3 grams

Instructions:

1. Heat olive oil in a skillet over medium heat. Add mushrooms and cook for 5-7 minutes until tender.
2. Add spinach and cook until wilted, about 2 minutes.
3. Serve the sautéed mushrooms and spinach over a bed of pre-cooked rice.

Why It's Great: This dish provides plant-based protein, fiber, and essential vitamins, making it both filling and nutritious.

Stuffed Portobello Mushrooms with Spinach and Feta

20 minutes

Ingredients:

- 2 large Portobello mushrooms, stems removed
- 1/2 cup fresh spinach
- 1/4 cup crumbled feta cheese
- 1 tablespoon olive oil
- Salt and pepper, to taste

Calories:	210
Protein:	8 grams
Carbohydrates:	5 grams
Fat:	18 grams
Fiber:	1 grams

Instructions:

1. Preheat oven to 400°F (200°C).
2. In a bowl, mix spinach and feta cheese.
3. Drizzle olive oil inside the mushrooms, and season with salt and pepper. Stuff each mushroom with the spinach and feta mixture.
4. Bake for 15 minutes until mushrooms are tender.

Why It's Great: This dish is a great source of plant-based protein and calcium, making it a flavorful and balanced dinner.

Note: This dish can be enjoyed as a light meal or paired with a salad or whole grains for a more substantial plate!

Broccoli and Almond Stir-Fry

15 minutes

Ingredients:

- 1 cup broccoli florets
- 1/4 cup sliced almonds
- 1 tablespoon olive oil
- Salt and pepper, to taste
- 1/2 teaspoon soy sauce (optional)

Calories:	190
Protein:	6 grams
Carbohydrates:	9 grams
Fat:	16 grams
Fiber:	4 grams

Instructions:

1. Heat olive oil in a skillet over medium heat. Add broccoli and cook for 5-7 minutes until tender-crisp.
2. Stir in sliced almonds and cook for another 1-2 minutes.
3. Season with salt, pepper, and soy sauce if desired.

Why It's Great: This stir-fry is simple, packed with fiber and healthy fats, and has a satisfying crunch from the almonds.

Note: For more substantial meal pair it with a protein source (like chicken or tofu) or grains (like quinoa or rice).

Zucchini and Chickpea Sauté with Fresh Herbs

15 minutes

Ingredients:

- 1 medium zucchini, sliced
- 1/2 cup canned chickpeas, rinsed and drained
- 1 tablespoon olive oil
- Salt and pepper, to taste
- Fresh basil or parsley, chopped, for garnish

Calories:	210
Protein:	6 grams
Carbohydrates:	19 grams
Fat:	12 grams
Fiber:	5 grams

Instructions:

1. Heat olive oil in a skillet over medium heat. Add zucchini slices and cook for 5-6 minutes until tender.
2. Add chickpeas and cook for an additional 2-3 minutes, stirring occasionally.
3. Season with salt and pepper and garnish with fresh herbs before serving.

Why It's Great: This dish is light, fresh, and full of fiber and plant-based protein, making it both filling and refreshing.

Sweet Potato Noodles with Pesto and Cherry Tomatoes

15 minutes

Ingredients:

- 1 medium sweet potato, spiralized
- 1/4 cup cherry tomatoes, halved
- 1 tablespoon pesto
- Salt and pepper, to taste

Calories:	210
Protein:	2 grams
Carbohydrates:	32 grams
Fat:	10 grams
Fiber:	5 grams

Instructions:

1. In a skillet, heat pesto over medium heat and add sweet potato noodles.
2. Cook for 5-6 minutes until the noodles are tender.
3. Add cherry tomatoes and toss until coated with pesto.
4. Season with salt and pepper before serving.

Why It's Great: This dish is colorful, nutrient-dense, and provides a healthy mix of carbs, fiber, and healthy fats.

Note: This dish is a well-rounded vegetarian option that's easy to prepare and packed with nutrients. For additional protein, consider adding grilled chicken, shrimp, or tofu.

Black Bean and Avocado Salad Bowl

10 minutes

Ingredients:

- 1/2 cup black beans, rinsed and drained
- 1/4 avocado, diced
- 1/4 cup cherry tomatoes, halved
- 1 tablespoon lime juice
- Salt and pepper, to taste

Calories:	180
Protein:	6 grams
Carbohydrates:	19 grams
Fat:	9 grams
Fiber:	7 grams

Instructions:

1. In a bowl, combine black beans, avocado, and cherry tomatoes.
2. Drizzle with lime juice and season with salt and pepper.
3. Toss gently to combine before serving.

Why It's Great: This bowl is rich in plant-based protein and healthy fats, providing a balanced, filling meal in minutes.

Spaghetti Squash with Marinara and Mushrooms

25 minutes

Ingredients:

- 1/2 small spaghetti squash
- 1/2 cup marinara sauce
- 1/4 cup mushrooms, sliced
- 1 tablespoon olive oil
- Salt and pepper, to taste

Calories:	185
Protein:	3 grams
Carbohydrates:	20 grams
Fat:	11 grams
Fiber:	4 grams

Instructions:

1. Microwave or bake the spaghetti squash until tender (about 10 minutes in the microwave or 25 minutes in the oven).
2. Scrape out the squash strands with a fork and set aside.
3. In a skillet, heat olive oil over medium heat, add mushrooms, and cook for 5-7 minutes until tender.
4. Serve the squash topped with marinara sauce and mushrooms.

Why It's Great: This dish is low in carbs, high in fiber, and provides a satisfying pasta-like experience without the heaviness.

Sautéed Cabbage with White Beans and Garlic

15 minutes

Ingredients:

- 1 cup shredded cabbage
- 1/2 cup white beans, rinsed and drained
- 1 clove garlic, minced
- 1 tablespoon olive oil
- Salt and pepper, to taste

Calories:	190
Protein:	6 grams
Carbohydrates:	18 grams
Fat:	11 grams
Fiber:	6 grams

Instructions:

1. Heat olive oil in a skillet over medium heat. Add garlic and cook for 1 minute until fragrant.
2. Add cabbage and cook for 5-7 minutes until slightly softened.
3. Stir in white beans and cook for another 2-3 minutes.
4. Season with salt and pepper before serving.

Why It's Great: This dish is packed with fiber, plant-based protein, and is quick and easy to make.

Roasted Vegetable Bowl with Hummus Dressing

25 minutes

Ingredients:

- 1/2 cup cauliflower florets
- 1/2 cup diced sweet potatoes
- 1/4 cup sliced bell peppers
- 1 tablespoon olive oil
- Salt and pepper, to taste
- 2 tablespoons hummus, thinned with a bit of water

Calories:	230
Protein:	4 grams
Carbohydrates:	26 grams
Fat:	13 grams
Fiber:	5 grams

Instructions:

1. Preheat oven to 400°F (200°C).
2. Toss cauliflower, sweet potatoes, and bell peppers with olive oil, salt, and pepper. Roast for 20-25 minutes until tender.
3. Serve veggies in a bowl and drizzle with hummus dressing.

Why It's Great: This bowl is colorful, nutrient-rich, and the hummus adds a creamy, flavorful dressing without heavy fats.

Tofu and Bell Pepper Stir-Fry with Ginger Soy Sauce

15 minutes

Ingredients:

- 1/2 cup firm tofu, cubed
- 1/2 bell pepper, sliced
- 1 tablespoon soy sauce
- 1/2 teaspoon grated ginger
- 1 tablespoon olive oil

Calories:	170
Protein:	8 grams
Carbohydrates:	5 grams
Fat:	13 grams
Fiber:	1 grams

Instructions:

1. In a skillet, heat olive oil over medium heat. Add tofu and cook for 3-4 minutes until golden.
2. Add bell pepper and ginger, and stir-fry for 3-4 more minutes.
3. Drizzle with soy sauce and serve.

Why It's Great: This stir-fry is rich in protein, with a flavorful boost from ginger and soy, making it filling and quick.

Note: Perfect as a quick meal or served alongside rice or noodles for a more filling option.

Chickpea Shawarma Bowl with Cucumber and Tzatziki

20 minutes

Ingredients:

- Mixed greens, for serving
- 1/2 cup canned chickpeas, rinsed and drained
- 1/2 teaspoon ground cumin
- 1/2 teaspoon paprika
- Salt and pepper, to taste
- 1/4 cup diced cucumber
- 2 tablespoons tzatziki sauce

Calories:	185
Protein:	6 grams
Carbohydrates:	20 grams
Fat:	9 grams
Fiber:	5 grams

Instructions:

1. In a skillet, heat a small amount of oil over medium heat. Add chickpeas, cumin, paprika, salt, and pepper. Cook for 5-6 minutes until chickpeas are slightly crispy.
2. In a bowl, layer mixed greens, spiced chickpeas, and cucumber.
3. Drizzle with tzatziki sauce before serving.

Why It's Great: This bowl is flavorful and filling, with plant-based protein, fiber, and a refreshing tzatziki drizzle.

Ratatouille with Chicken and Fresh Herbs

25 minutes

141

Ingredients:

- 1 small chicken breast, diced
- 1/2 cup zucchini, sliced
- 1/2 cup eggplant, diced
- 1/4 cup bell pepper, diced
- 1/4 cup diced tomatoes
- 1 tablespoon olive oil
- 1 clove garlic, minced
- Salt and pepper, to taste
- Fresh basil or thyme, chopped

Calories:	274
Protein:	30 grams
Carbohydrates:	7 grams
Fat:	17 grams
Fiber:	3 grams

Instructions:

1. Heat half the olive oil in a large skillet over medium-high heat. Add the diced chicken, season with salt and pepper, and sauté for 5-7 minutes until fully cooked and golden brown. Remove the chicken from the skillet and set aside.
2. In the same skillet, add the remaining olive oil and minced garlic. Sauté for 30 seconds until fragrant. Add the zucchini, eggplant, and bell pepper, and cook for 5 minutes until slightly tender.
3. Add the diced tomatoes to the skillet and return the cooked chicken to the pan. Stir well, lower the heat, and let it simmer for 5 minutes to blend the flavors.
4. Garnish with fresh herbs before serving.

Why It's Great: This dish is rich in fiber, vitamins, and antioxidants, providing a comforting, plant-based dinner.

Baked & Roasted Dishes

Baked Chicken with Brussels Sprouts and Sweet Potatoes

25 minutes

Ingredients:

- 1 chicken breast, cubed
- 1/2 cup Brussels sprouts
- 1/2 cup sweet potato, diced
- 1 tablespoon olive oil
- Salt and pepper, to taste
- 1/2 teaspoon paprika

Calories:	325
Protein:	30 grams
Carbohydrates:	19 grams
Fat:	17 grams
Fiber:	4 grams

Instructions:

1. Preheat oven to 400°F (200°C).
2. Toss chicken, Brussels sprouts, and sweet potato with olive oil, salt, pepper, and paprika.
3. Spread everything on a baking sheet and bake for 20-25 minutes until the chicken is cooked through and vegetables are tender.

Why It's Great: This dish is a balanced meal with lean protein, fiber, and complex carbs, all roasted for a warm, satisfying flavor.

Stuffed Zucchini Boats with Ground Turkey and Marinara

25 minutes

Ingredients:

- 2 medium zucchinis, halved and hollowed out
- 1/2 cup ground turkey
- 1/4 cup marinara sauce
- Salt and pepper, to taste
- 1/4 cup mozzarella cheese

Calories:	318
Protein:	31 grams
Carbohydrates:	14 grams
Fat:	15 grams
Fiber:	3 grams

Instructions:

1. Preheat oven to 375°F (190°C).
2. In a skillet, cook ground turkey over medium heat until browned, seasoning with salt and pepper.
3. Spoon the turkey into the hollowed zucchini halves and top with marinara sauce and shredded cheese.
4. Bake for 15-20 minutes until the cheese is melted and bubbly.

Why It's Great: This dish is low in carbs, high in protein, and has a delicious Italian-inspired flavor.

Broccoli and Cheese Stuffed Chicken Breast

25 minutes

Ingredients:

- 1 chicken breast, butterflied
- 1/4 cup broccoli florets, chopped
- 2 tablespoons shredded cheddar cheese
- Salt and pepper, to taste
- 1 tablespoon olive oil

Calories:	303
Protein:	30 grams
Carbohydrates:	2 grams
Fat:	21 grams
Fiber:	1 grams

Instructions:

1. Preheat oven to 375°F (190°C).
2. Stuff the butterflied chicken breast with broccoli and cheddar cheese. Secure with toothpicks if necessary.
3. Season the outside with salt and pepper.
4. Heat olive oil in a skillet over medium heat, searing the chicken for 2-3 minutes per side, then transfer to the oven for 15-20 minutes until fully cooked.

Why It's Great: This dish combines lean protein with a dose of fiber and vitamins from the broccoli, with a comforting touch of melted cheese.

Lemon Garlic Roasted Chicken Thighs with Asparagus

25 minutes

Ingredients:

- 1 chicken thigh, bone-in, skin-on
- 1/4 lemon, sliced
- 1/2 clove garlic, minced
- 1/2 tablespoon olive oil
- Salt and pepper, to taste
- 1/2 cup asparagus, trimmed

Calories:	280
Protein:	19 grams
Carbohydrates:	4 grams
Fat:	21 grams
Fiber:	2 grams

Instructions:

1. Preheat oven to 400°F (200°C).
2. Rub chicken thighs with olive oil, garlic, salt, and pepper. Place lemon slices on top.
3. Arrange chicken thighs and asparagus on a baking sheet.
4. Roast for 20-25 minutes until the chicken is golden and fully cooked.

Why It's Great: This dish is easy to prepare, packed with flavor, and provides a balance of protein, fiber, and healthy fats.

Lemon Dill Trout with Steamed Green Beans

20 minutes

Ingredients:

- 1 trout fillet
- Salt and pepper, to taste
- 1/2 lemon, sliced
- Fresh dill, for garnish
- 1 cup green beans, trimmed

Calories:	255
Protein:	25 grams
Carbohydrates:	10 grams
Fat:	14 grams
Fiber:	4 grams

Instructions:

1. Preheat oven to 400°F (200°C).
2. Season trout with salt and pepper, and place lemon slices on top.
3. Bake for 15 minutes until the trout is flaky.
4. Steam green beans while the trout bakes.
5. Garnish with fresh dill and serve.

Why It's Great: This dish is light and full of protein, omega-3s, and vitamins from the fresh green beans.

Sheet Pan Shrimp with Zucchini and Bell Peppers

20 minutes

Ingredients:

- 1/2 lb shrimp, peeled and deveined
- 1 small zucchini, sliced
- 1/2 bell pepper, sliced
- 1 tablespoon olive oil
- Salt and pepper, to taste
- 1/2 teaspoon paprika

Calories:	249
Protein:	22 grams
Carbohydrates:	9 grams
Fat:	15 grams
Fiber:	3 grams

Instructions:

1. Preheat oven to 400°F (200°C).
2. Toss shrimp, zucchini, and bell pepper with olive oil, salt, pepper, and paprika.
3. Spread everything on a baking sheet and roast for 10-12 minutes until shrimp is pink and veggies are tender.

Why It's Great: This dish is high in protein, low in carbs, and easy to prepare, perfect for a quick dinner.

Roasted Cauliflower and Chickpea Bowl

25 minutes

Ingredients:

- 1 cup cauliflower florets
- 1/2 cup canned chickpeas, rinsed and drained
- 1 tablespoon olive oil
- 1/2 teaspoon cumin
- Salt and pepper, to taste

Calories:	278
Protein:	9 grams
Carbohydrates:	27 grams
Fat:	16 grams
Fiber:	8 grams

Instructions:

1. Preheat oven to 400°F (200°C).
2. Toss cauliflower and chickpeas with olive oil, cumin, salt, and pepper.
3. Roast on a baking sheet for 20-25 minutes until golden and crispy.
4. Serve in a bowl and enjoy.

Why It's Great: This dish is packed with fiber and plant-based protein, making it filling and nutritious.

Italian-Style Stuffed Zucchini with Herbs

25 minutes – Precooked ingredients required

Ingredients:

- 2 medium zucchinis, halved and hollowed out
- 1/4 cup diced tomatoes
- 1/4 cup cooked quinoa or rice
- 1/2 teaspoon dried basil
- 1/2 teaspoon dried oregano
- Salt and pepper, to taste
- 1 tablespoon Parmesan cheese

Calories:	122
Protein:	7 grams
Carbohydrates:	19 grams
Fat:	3 grams
Fiber:	4 grams

Instructions:

1. Preheat oven to 375°F (190°C).
2. In a bowl, combine diced tomatoes, quinoa (or rice), basil, oregano, salt, and pepper.
3. Stuff the zucchini halves with the mixture and sprinkle with Parmesan cheese.
4. Bake for 20-25 minutes until zucchini is tender.

Why It's Great: This dish is low-carb and packed with flavor, perfect for a light yet satisfying dinner.

Herb-Roasted Chicken with Baby Carrots

25 minutes

Ingredients:

- 1 chicken breast
- 1/2 teaspoon dried thyme
- 1/2 teaspoon dried rosemary
- Salt and pepper, to taste
- 1 cup baby carrots
- 1 tablespoon olive oil

Calories:	289
Protein:	27 grams
Carbohydrates:	12 grams
Fat:	17 grams
Fiber:	4 grams

Instructions:

1. Preheat oven to 400°F (200°C).
2. Rub chicken with thyme, rosemary, salt, and pepper.
3. Toss baby carrots with olive oil, salt, and pepper.
4. Place chicken and carrots on a baking sheet and roast for 20-25 minutes until the chicken is fully cooked.

Why It's Great: This meal is wholesome and balanced, with lean protein and fiber-rich carrots.

Lemon Pepper Tilapia with Roasted Asparagus

20 minutes

Ingredients:

- 1 tilapia fillet
- Salt and pepper, to taste
- 1/2 teaspoon lemon zest
- 1 cup asparagus, trimmed
- 1 tablespoon olive oil

Calories:	257
Protein:	26 grams
Carbohydrates:	5 grams
Fat:	16 grams
Fiber:	3 grams

Instructions:

1. Preheat oven to 400°F (200°C).
2. Season tilapia with salt, pepper, and lemon zest.
3. Place tilapia and asparagus on a baking sheet. Drizzle asparagus with olive oil, salt, and pepper.
4. Bake for 15-20 minutes until tilapia is flaky and asparagus is tender.

Why It's Great: This dish is light, high in protein, and packed with flavor from the lemon zest and fresh asparagus.

Baked Turkey Meatballs with Green Beans

25 minutes

Ingredients:

- 1/2 lb ground turkey
- 1/4 cup breadcrumbs (optional)
- 1/2 teaspoon garlic powder
- Salt and pepper, to taste
- 1 cup green beans, trimmed
- 1 tablespoon olive oil

Calories:	430
Protein:	27 grams
Carbohydrates:	27 grams
Fat:	24 grams
Fiber:	4 grams

Instructions:

1. Preheat oven to 400°F (200°C).
2. In a bowl, mix ground turkey, breadcrumbs, garlic powder, salt, and pepper. Form into small meatballs.
3. Place meatballs and green beans on a baking sheet. Drizzle green beans with olive oil and season with salt and pepper.
4. Bake for 20-25 minutes until meatballs are cooked through and green beans are tender.

Why It's Great: This dish provides lean protein and fiber, with a comforting, oven-baked flavor.

Roasted Brussels Sprouts and Carrots with Balsamic Glaze

25 minutes

Ingredients:

- 1/2 cup Brussels sprouts, halved
- 1/2 cup carrots, sliced
- 1 tablespoon olive oil
- Salt and pepper, to taste
- 1 tablespoon balsamic vinegar

Calories:	186
Protein:	3 grams
Carbohydrates:	14 grams
Fat:	14 grams
Fiber:	4 grams

Instructions:

1. Preheat oven to 400°F (200°C).
2. Toss Brussels sprouts and carrots with olive oil, salt, and pepper.
3. Roast on a baking sheet for 20-25 minutes until tender.
4. Drizzle with balsamic vinegar before serving.

Why It's Great: This dish is nutrient-dense, high in fiber, and has a delicious balance of savory and sweet.

One-Pan Baked Sausage and Peppers

20 minutes

Ingredients:

- 1 sausage link (such as chicken or turkey sausage), sliced
- 1/2 bell pepper, sliced
- 1/4 onion, sliced
- 1 tablespoon olive oil
- Salt and pepper, to taste

Calories:	299
Protein:	14 grams
Carbohydrates:	8 grams
Fat:	25 grams
Fiber:	2 grams

Instructions:

1. Preheat oven to 400°F (200°C).
2. Toss sausage, bell pepper, and onion with olive oil, salt, and pepper.
3. Spread everything on a baking sheet and bake for 15-20 minutes until sausage is cooked and peppers are tender.

Why It's Great: This meal is quick, filling, and balanced with protein and veggies, perfect for a busy evening.

Roasted Cauliflower Steaks with Garlic and Herbs

25 minutes

Ingredients:

- 1 head cauliflower, sliced into thick "steaks"
- 1 tablespoon olive oil
- 1 clove garlic, minced
- Salt and pepper, to taste
- Fresh thyme or rosemary, for garnish

Calories:	273
Protein:	12 grams
Carbohydrates:	31 grams
Fat:	15 grams
Fiber:	12 grams

Instructions:

1. Preheat oven to 400°F (200°C).
2. Brush cauliflower steaks with olive oil, garlic, salt, and pepper.
3. Place on a baking sheet and roast for 20-25 minutes until golden and tender.
4. Garnish with fresh herbs before serving.

Why It's Great: This dish is hearty, nutritious, and packed with fiber and vitamins. The cauliflower provides a satisfying base, while the garlic and herbs enhance the flavor.

Parmesan-Crusted Cod with Broccoli

20 minutes

Ingredients:

- 1 cod fillet
- Salt and pepper, to taste
- 1 tablespoon grated Parmesan cheese
- 1 cup broccoli florets
- 1 tablespoon olive oil

Calories:	261
Protein:	23 grams
Carbohydrates:	6 grams
Fat:	16 grams
Fiber:	2 grams

Instructions:

1. Preheat oven to 400°F (200°C).
2. Season cod with salt and pepper and sprinkle with Parmesan cheese.
3. Toss broccoli with olive oil, salt, and pepper. Arrange cod and broccoli on a baking sheet.
4. Bake for 15-20 minutes until cod is flaky and broccoli is tender.

Why It's Great: This dish provides lean protein and healthy fats, with the Parmesan adding a savory, cheesy touch.

Mediterranean Baked Chicken with Olives and Tomatoes

25 minutes

Ingredients:

- 1 chicken breast
- 1/4 cup cherry tomatoes, halved
- 1/4 cup Kalamata olives, pitted
- 1 tablespoon olive oil
- Salt and pepper, to taste
- Fresh basil, for garnish

Calories:	336
Protein:	27 grams
Carbohydrates:	4 grams
Fat:	26 grams
Fiber:	0 grams

Instructions:

1. Preheat oven to 400°F (200°C).
2. Season chicken with salt and pepper. Place chicken, cherry tomatoes, and olives in a baking dish. Drizzle with olive oil.
3. Bake for 20-25 minutes until chicken is cooked through.
4. Garnish with fresh basil before serving.

Why It's Great: This dish is rich in flavor, with protein from the chicken and healthy fats from the olives.

Sweet Potato and Zucchini Bake with Garlic and Thyme

25 minutes

Ingredients:

- 1 small sweet potato, sliced
- 1 small zucchini, sliced
- 1 tablespoon olive oil
- Salt and pepper, to taste
- 1/2 teaspoon dried thyme

Calories:	251
Protein:	4 grams
Carbohydrates:	30 grams
Fat:	14 grams
Fiber:	5 grams

Instructions:

1. Preheat oven to 400°F (200°C).
2. Toss sweet potato and zucchini slices with olive oil, salt, pepper, and thyme.
3. Arrange on a baking sheet and bake for 20-25 minutes until tender.

Why It's Great: This dish is a comforting, nutrient-rich side that's high in fiber, vitamins, and minerals.

One-Pan Chicken and Mushroom Bake

25 minutes

Ingredients:

- 1 chicken breast, cut into cubes
- 1/2 cup mushrooms, sliced
- 1 tablespoon olive oil
- Salt and pepper, to taste
- 1/2 teaspoon dried rosemary

Calories:	247
Protein:	27 grams
Carbohydrates:	2 grams
Fat:	17 grams
Fiber:	1 grams

Instructions:

1. Preheat oven to 400°F (200°C).
2. Toss chicken and mushrooms with olive oil, salt, pepper, and rosemary.
3. Spread on a baking sheet and bake for 20-25 minutes until the chicken is cooked through and mushrooms are tender.

Why It's Great: This dish is simple and flavorful, featuring tender chicken paired with earthy mushrooms. It's rich in protein, making it a satisfying option for a quick and healthy meal. The rosemary adds a touch of aromatic depth to elevate the flavors.

Baked Eggplant Parmesan (light on cheese)

25 minutes

Ingredients:

- 1 small eggplant, sliced
- 1/2 cup marinara sauce
- 1/4 cup grated Parmesan cheese
- 1 tablespoon olive oil
- Salt and pepper, to taste

Calories:	319
Protein:	12 grams
Carbohydrates:	21 grams
Fat:	21 grams
Fiber:	9 grams

Instructions:

1. Preheat oven to 400°F (200°C).
2. Arrange eggplant slices on a baking sheet, drizzle with olive oil, and season with salt and pepper.
3. Bake for 15 minutes, then top with marinara sauce and sprinkle with Parmesan cheese.
4. Bake for an additional 5-10 minutes until cheese is melted and eggplant is tender.

Why It's Great: This lighter take on eggplant Parmesan is full of flavor without being too heavy, offering fiber and antioxidants.

Low-Carb Bowls

Zucchini Noodles with Bolognese Sauce
25 minutes

Ingredients:

- 1 medium zucchini, spiralized
- 1/2 lb ground beef or turkey
- 1/2 cup marinara sauce
- 1 tablespoon olive oil
- Salt and pepper, to taste
- Fresh basil, for garnish

Calories:	357
Protein:	25 grams
Carbohydrates:	13 grams
Fat:	23 grams
Fiber:	4 grams

Instructions:

1. In a skillet, heat olive oil over medium heat and add ground beef or turkey. Cook until browned, about 5-7 minutes.
2. Stir in marinara sauce and simmer for 5 minutes.
3. Meanwhile, sauté zucchini noodles in a separate pan for 2-3 minutes until slightly tender.
4. Serve the Bolognese sauce over the zucchini noodles and garnish with fresh basil.

Why It's Great: This bowl is low in carbs but high in protein and flavor, making it a satisfying alternative to traditional pasta dishes.

Cauliflower Rice with Sautéed Shrimp

20 minutes

Ingredients:

- 1 cup cauliflower rice (fresh or frozen)
- 1/2 lb shrimp, peeled and deveined
- 1 tablespoon olive oil
- 1 clove garlic, minced
- Salt and pepper, to taste

Calories:	238
Protein:	22 grams
Carbohydrates:	6 grams
Fat:	15 grams
Fiber:	2 grams

Instructions:

1. Heat olive oil in a skillet over medium heat. Add garlic and cook for 1 minute until fragrant.
2. Add shrimp and cook for 3-4 minutes until pink and cooked through. Remove from the skillet and set aside.
3. In the same skillet, add cauliflower rice and sauté for 5-7 minutes until tender. Season with salt and pepper.
4. Serve the sautéed shrimp over cauliflower rice.

Why It's Great: This dish is low in carbs and calories, providing a great source of protein and fiber.

Greek Bowl with Chicken, Cucumber, and Tzatziki

20 minutes

Ingredients:

- 1 chicken breast, grilled and sliced
- 1/2 cucumber, diced
- 1/4 cup cherry tomatoes, halved
- 2 tablespoons tzatziki sauce
- 1 tablespoon olive oil
- Salt and pepper, to taste

Calories:	284
Protein:	17 grams
Carbohydrates:	5 grams
Fat:	19 grams
Fiber:	1 grams

Instructions:

1. Grill the chicken breast until fully cooked and slice.
2. In a bowl, layer sliced chicken, diced cucumber, and cherry tomatoes.
3. Drizzle with olive oil and season with salt and pepper. Top with tzatziki sauce.

Why It's Great: This bowl is refreshing and packed with lean protein, making it a perfect light dinner.

Egg Roll in a Bowl with Ground Turkey

20 minutes

Ingredients:

- 1/2 lb ground turkey
- 1 cup coleslaw mix (shredded cabbage and carrots)
- 1 tablespoon soy sauce
- 1 teaspoon sesame oil
- Green onions, for garnish

Calories:	245
Protein:	24 grams
Carbohydrates:	6 grams
Fat:	14 grams
Fiber:	2 grams

Instructions:

1. In a skillet, cook ground turkey over medium heat until browned.
2. Add coleslaw mix, soy sauce, and sesame oil. Sauté for 5-7 minutes until the veggies are tender.
3. Garnish with chopped green onions before serving.

Why It's Great: This dish is low in carbs and full of flavor, with lean protein and lots of vegetables.

Pesto Zoodles with Cherry Tomatoes and Mozzarella

20 minutes

Ingredients:

- 1 medium zucchini, spiralized
- 1/2 cup cherry tomatoes, halved
- 1/4 cup mozzarella balls (bocconcini)
- 2 tablespoons pesto
- Salt and pepper, to taste

Calories:	292
Protein:	11 grams
Carbohydrates:	13 grams
Fat:	23 grams
Fiber:	3 grams

Instructions:

1. In a skillet, sauté zucchini noodles for 2-3 minutes until slightly tender.
2. Stir in cherry tomatoes and cook for another 2 minutes.
3. Remove from heat, add mozzarella balls and pesto, and toss to combine.
4. Season with salt and pepper before serving.

Why It's Great: This dish is low in carbs and packed with flavor, making it a fresh and satisfying meal.

Buffalo Cauliflower Rice with Grilled Chicken

25 minutes

Ingredients:

- 1 cup cauliflower rice (fresh or frozen)
- 1 chicken breast (4 oz)
- 2 tablespoons buffalo sauce
- 1 tablespoon olive oil
- Celery sticks, for serving

Calories:	341
Protein:	25 grams
Carbohydrates:	7 grams
Fat:	15 grams
Fiber:	2 grams

Instructions:

1. Grill and slice chicken.
2. In a skillet, heat olive oil over medium heat. Add cauliflower rice and sauté for 5-7 minutes.
3. Stir in buffalo sauce and cook for another minute.
4. Serve cauliflower rice topped with grilled chicken and celery sticks on the side.

Why It's Great: This bowl is low-carb and packed with protein, with a spicy kick from the buffalo sauce.

Mediterranean Shrimp Bowl with Olives and Feta

25 minutes

Ingredients:

- 1/4 lb shrimp (3-4 oz), peeled and deveined
- 2 tablespoons olives
- 2 tablespoons cherry tomatoes
- 1 tablespoon feta cheese
- 1/2 tablespoon olive oil
- Salt and pepper, to taste

Calories:	191
Protein:	13 grams
Carbohydrates:	3 grams
Fat:	15 grams
Fiber:	1 grams

Instructions:

1. Heat olive oil in a skillet over medium heat and cook shrimp for 3-4 minutes until pink.
2. In a bowl, combine shrimp, pitted and sliced olives, halved cherry tomatoes, and crumbled feta cheese.
3. Season with salt and pepper before serving.

Why It's Great: This bowl is high in protein and healthy fats, making it a satisfying meal packed with flavor.

Chipotle Chicken and Cauliflower Rice Bowl

25 minutes

Ingredients:

- 1/4 lb chicken breast, diced
- 1/2 cup cauliflower rice
- 1/2 tablespoon chipotle sauce
- 1/4 cup black beans, rinsed and drained
- 1/8 avocado, sliced
- Salt and pepper, to taste

Calories:	310
Protein:	27 grams
Carbohydrates:	15 grams
Fat:	10 grams
Fiber:	7 grams

Instructions:

1. In a skillet, cook diced chicken until browned. Stir in chipotle sauce and cook for an additional 2-3 minutes.
2. In a separate pan, sauté cauliflower rice for 5-7 minutes until tender.
3. Serve the chipotle chicken over cauliflower rice, topped with black beans and avocado.

Why It's Great: This bowl is high in protein and fiber while being low in carbs, with a satisfying spicy flavor.

Asian-Inspired Tofu and Cabbage Bowl

20 minutes

Ingredients:

- 1/2 block firm tofu, cubed
- 1 cup cabbage, shredded
- 1 tablespoon soy sauce
- 1 tablespoon sesame oil
- Salt and pepper, to taste
- Sesame seeds, for garnish

Calories:	296
Protein:	17 grams
Carbohydrates:	9 grams
Fat:	22 grams
Fiber:	3 grams

Instructions:

1. In a skillet, heat sesame oil over medium heat. Add tofu cubes and cook until golden on all sides, about 8-10 minutes.
2. Add cabbage and soy sauce, and cook until cabbage is wilted, about 3-4 minutes.
3. Serve topped with sesame seeds.

Why It's Great: This bowl is rich in plant-based protein and fiber, offering a delicious and satisfying meal.

Avocado Chicken Salad Bowl

15 minutes

Ingredients:

- Mixed greens, for serving

- 1 chicken breast, cooked and shredded
- 1/2 avocado, mashed
- 1 tablespoon Greek yogurt (optional)
- 1/4 cup diced celery
- Salt and pepper, to taste

Calories:	261
Protein:	29 grams
Carbohydrates:	9 grams
Fat:	14 grams
Fiber:	6 grams

Instructions:

1. In a bowl, combine shredded chicken, mashed avocado, Greek yogurt, celery, salt, and pepper.
2. Serve the chicken salad over a bed of mixed greens.

Why It's Great: This bowl is creamy and full of flavor while being high in protein and healthy fats, making it a filling option.

Sautéed Spinach and Mushroom Cauliflower Rice Bowl

20 minutes

Ingredients:

- 1 cup cauliflower rice (fresh or frozen)
- 1 cup spinach
- 1/2 cup mushrooms, sliced
- 1 tablespoon olive oil
- Salt and pepper, to taste

Calories:	159
Protein:	4 grams
Carbohydrates:	8 grams
Fat:	14 grams
Fiber:	3 grams

Instructions:

1. In a skillet, heat olive oil over medium heat. Add mushrooms and cook for 5-6 minutes until tender.
2. Stir in spinach and cook until wilted, about 2 minutes.
3. In a separate pan, sauté cauliflower rice for 5-7 minutes until tender.
4. Serve the sautéed spinach and mushrooms over the cauliflower rice.

Why It's Great: This dish is packed with fiber, vitamins, and minerals, providing a healthy and low-carb option.

Thai Chicken and Cucumber Salad Bowl

15 minutes

Ingredients:

- 1 chicken breast, cooked and sliced
- 1/2 cucumber, thinly sliced
- 1/4 cup shredded carrots
- 2 tablespoons peanut sauce
- Fresh cilantro, for garnish

Calories:	228
Protein:	30 grams
Carbohydrates:	8 grams
Fat:	10 grams
Fiber:	2 grams

Instructions:

1. In a bowl, layer sliced chicken, cucumber, and shredded carrots.
2. Drizzle with peanut sauce and toss gently.
3. Garnish with fresh cilantro before serving.

Why It's Great: This bowl is refreshing and full of protein, with a deliciously nutty flavor from the peanut sauce.

Spicy Beef and Cauliflower Rice Bowl

25 minutes

Ingredients:

- 1/4 lb ground beef
- 1/2 cup cauliflower rice
- 1/2 tablespoon chili paste or sriracha
- Salt and pepper, to taste
- Sliced green onions, for garnish

Calories:	217
Protein:	15 grams
Carbohydrates:	4 grams
Fat:	15 grams
Fiber:	1 grams

Instructions:

1. In a skillet, cook ground beef over medium heat until browned. Drain excess fat if necessary.
2. Stir in chili paste, salt, and pepper, and cook for an additional 2-3 minutes.
3. In a separate pan, sauté cauliflower rice for 5-7 minutes until tender.
4. Serve the spicy beef over cauliflower rice, garnished with sliced green onions.

Why It's Great: This dish offers a kick of spice along with protein and fiber, making it a filling option without the carbs.

Salmon and Avocado Bowl with Mixed Greens

20 minutes

Ingredients:

- 1 small salmon fillet
- 1/2 avocado, sliced
- 1 cup mixed greens
- 1/2 tablespoon olive oil
- Salt and pepper, to taste

Calories:	333
Protein:	16 grams
Carbohydrates:	7 grams
Fat:	27 grams
Fiber:	6 grams

Instructions:

1. Season salmon with salt and pepper and cook in a skillet over medium heat for 4-5 minutes per side until cooked through.
2. In a bowl, place mixed greens and top with salmon and avocado slices.
3. Drizzle with olive oil before serving.

Why It's Great: This bowl is rich in omega-3 fatty acids, healthy fats, and vitamins, making it both satisfying and nutritious.

Mediterranean Eggplant and Greek Yogurt Bowl

25 minutes

Ingredients:

- 1 small eggplant, diced
- 1 tablespoon olive oil
- 2 tablespoons Greek yogurt
- Salt and pepper, to taste
- Fresh parsley, chopped, for garnish

Calories:	255
Protein:	5 grams
Carbohydrates:	15 grams
Fat:	20 grams
Fiber:	9 grams

Instructions:

1. Preheat the oven to 400°F (200°C). Toss diced eggplant with olive oil, salt, and pepper. Spread on a baking sheet.
2. Roast for 20-25 minutes until tender and golden.
3. Plate the roasted eggplant and top with a dollop of Greek yogurt. Garnish with fresh parsley.
4. Serve immediately and enjoy this refreshing, nutrient-packed dish.

Why It's Great: This dish is rich in fiber and flavor, providing a satisfying and healthy low-carb option.

Lemon Dill Tofu Bowl with Spinach

20 minutes

Ingredients:

- 1/2 block firm tofu, cubed
- 1 cup spinach
- 1 tablespoon lemon juice
- 1/2 teaspoon dried dill
- Salt and pepper, to taste

Calories:	158
Protein:	16 grams
Carbohydrates:	6 grams
Fat:	8 grams
Fiber:	2 grams

Instructions:

1. In a skillet, sauté tofu cubes until golden on all sides, about 8-10 minutes. Stir in lemon juice, dill, salt, and pepper.
2. Add spinach and cook until wilted, about 2 minutes.
3. Serve tofu and spinach in a bowl.

Why It's Great: This dish is high in protein, packed with nutrients, and light, making it a perfect dinner option.

Greek Yogurt, Cucumber, and Quinoa Bowl with Mint

10 minutes – Precooked ingredients required

Ingredients:

- 1/2 cup cooked quinoa
- 1/4 cup Greek yogurt
- 1/4 cup cucumber, diced
- 2 oz canned tuna
- Fresh mint, chopped, for garnish
- Salt and pepper, to taste

Calories:	267
Protein:	25 grams
Carbohydrates:	17 grams
Fat:	9 grams
Fiber:	2 grams

Instructions:

1. Combine the cooked quinoa, diced cucumber, and canned tuna in a bowl.
2. Add Greek yogurt and mix lightly to coat the ingredients evenly.
3. Season with salt, pepper, and garnish with fresh mint.

Why It's Great: This dish is packed with protein and offers a refreshing, cooling flavor, perfect for a light dinner.

Garlic and Lemon Chicken over Cauliflower Rice

25 minutes

Ingredients:

- 1 chicken breast, diced
- 1 cup cauliflower rice (fresh or frozen)
- 1 tablespoon olive oil
- 1 clove garlic, minced
- Juice of 1/2 lemon
- Salt and pepper, to taste

Calories:	272
Protein:	28 grams
Carbohydrates:	7 grams
Fat:	17 grams
Fiber:	2 grams

Instructions:

1. In a skillet, heat olive oil over medium heat. Add garlic and cook for 1 minute until fragrant.
2. Add diced chicken and cook until browned and cooked through, about 5-7 minutes.
3. Stir in lemon juice and season with salt and pepper.
4. In a separate pan, sauté cauliflower rice for 5-7 minutes until tender, and serve the chicken over it.

Why It's Great: This dish combines lean protein with cauliflower rice for a low-carb, flavorful meal that's quick to prepare.

Chapter 7

Desserts

Desserts often hold a special place in our hearts and can be a delightful way to conclude a meal. However, when it comes to maintaining energy levels and supporting overall health, it's important to choose desserts that not only satisfy your sweet tooth but also nourish your body. In the Good Energy Diet, desserts are crafted to be both enjoyable and beneficial, featuring ingredients that promote sustained energy rather than causing sugar crashes.

The key to a satisfying dessert lies in its composition. Opting for options that include whole, natural ingredients—such as fruits, nuts, and whole grains—can provide essential nutrients while keeping added sugars in check. These healthier alternatives can help you feel fulfilled without sacrificing your energy levels. For instance, desserts made with fruits can offer natural sweetness along with vitamins, minerals, and fiber that contribute to overall well-being.

Timing is also important when it comes to enjoying desserts. While it's tempting to indulge after every meal, it's best to consider your daily energy needs and how desserts fit into your overall nutritional plan. A well-timed treat can serve as a mid-afternoon pick-me-up or a rewarding end to a healthy dinner, helping you maintain balance throughout your day.

In this chapter, you'll discover a variety of dessert recipes that align with the principles of the Good Energy Diet. These recipes are designed to provide satisfaction while supporting your health goals, making them perfect for any occasion. From fruity delights to nutritious treats, these desserts will prove that you can indulge without compromising your energy or wellness. Let's dive in and explore the delicious possibilities!

No-Cook Good Energy Desserts

---

1. **Greek Yogurt Cups** - Individual servings of Greek yogurt topped with honey or fruit.
2. **Fruit Cups** - Pre-packaged cups of mixed fresh fruit.
3. **Chia Seed Pudding Cups** - Store-bought chia pudding made with almond milk and sweeteners.
4. **Nut Butter Packets** - Single-serve nut butter packets to dip fruits like apples or bananas.
5. **Dark Chocolate Bars** - High-quality dark chocolate for a satisfying treat.
6. **Granola Bars** - Store-bought bars made with oats, nuts, and dried fruits.
7. **Rice Cakes with Nut Butter** - Pre-packaged rice cakes that can be topped with nut butter.
8. **Energy Bites** - Store-bought energy bites made with oats, nuts, and honey.
9. **Coconut Yogurt** - Dairy-free yogurt made from coconut milk, often found in individual servings.
10. **Protein Bars** - Convenient bars that provide protein and energy, choose lower sugar options.
11. **Dried Fruit** - A variety of dried fruits such as apricots, figs, or mango.
12. **Frozen Fruit Bars** - Fruit popsicles made from pureed fruit without added sugars.
13. **Almonds or Mixed Nuts** - Conveniently packaged for on-the-go snacking.
14. **Cottage Cheese Cups** - Individual servings of cottage cheese that can be topped with fruit or honey.
15. **Dark Chocolate-Covered Almonds** - A great combination of healthy fats and antioxidants.
16. **Yogurt Parfaits** - Pre-made parfaits with layers of yogurt, granola, and fruit.
17. **Protein Smoothies** - Bottled smoothies that contain protein and healthy ingredients.
18. **Frozen Grapes** - Grab and go bags of frozen grapes for a refreshing treat.
19. **Apple Slices with Caramel Dip** - Pre-packaged apple slices that come with a small container of caramel dip.
20. **Coconut Chips** - Crunchy, lightly sweetened coconut chips for a tropical snack.
21. **Graham Crackers with Nut Butter** - Individual packs of graham crackers that can be topped with nut butter.
22. **Mini Cheesecakes** - Individual mini cheesecakes found in grocery store bakeries.
23. **Banana Chips** - Crunchy banana chips for a sweet, crunchy treat.
24. **Almond Milk Chocolate Pudding Cups** - Dairy-free chocolate pudding in single servings.
25. **Chocolate-Covered Rice Cakes** - Light and crispy rice cakes topped with chocolate.
26. **Nutty Protein Balls** - Pre-made protein balls available at health food stores, made with oats and nuts.

Good Energy Desserts (Light Cooking)

Banana Oatmeal Pancakes

15 minutes

Ingredients:

- 1 ripe banana, mashed
- 1/2 cup rolled oats (or quick oats)
- 2 large eggs
- 1/4 teaspoon vanilla extract (optional)
- 1/4 teaspoon baking powder (optional, for fluffier pancakes)
- Pinch of cinnamon (optional)
- Butter or oil, for greasing the pan

Calories:	195
Protein:	9 grams
Carbohydrates:	27 grams
Fat:	5 grams
Fiber:	3 grams

Instructions:

1. In a blender or mixing bowl, combine the banana, oats, eggs, vanilla extract, baking powder, and cinnamon. Blend until smooth or mix well for a slightly textured batter.
2. Heat a non-stick skillet or griddle over medium heat. Grease lightly with butter or oil.
3. Pour 2-3 tablespoons of batter per pancake onto the skillet. Cook for 2-3 minutes until bubbles form on the surface, then flip and cook for another 1-2 minutes until golden brown.
4. Stack the pancakes on a plate and serve with your favorite toppings, such as fresh fruit, Greek yogurt, maple syrup, or peanut butter.

Chocolate Chia Seed Pudding

5 minutes – Overnight cooking

Ingredients:

- 2 tablespoons chia seeds
- 1/2 cup almond milk
- 1 tablespoon unsweetened cocoa powder
- 1 teaspoon maple syrup, honey, or sweetener of choice
- 1/4 teaspoon vanilla extract (optional)

Calories:	195
Protein:	9 grams
Carbohydrates:	27 grams
Fat:	5 grams
Fiber:	3 grams

Instructions:

1. In a small bowl or jar, combine the chia seeds, almond milk, cocoa powder, maple syrup, and vanilla extract (if using). Stir well to ensure the cocoa powder is fully mixed and there are no lumps.
2. Cover and refrigerate for at least 2 hours or overnight. Stir once after 30 minutes to redistribute the chia seeds evenly.
3. Once the pudding has thickened, give it a good stir and serve topped with fresh berries, nuts, coconut flakes, or a dollop of Greek yogurt if desired.

Baked Apples with Cinnamon

25 minutes

Ingredients:

- 1 medium apple, cored
- 1 teaspoon cinnamon
- 1/2 teaspoon maple syrup or honey (optional)
- 1 teaspoon chopped nuts
- 1 teaspoon raisins (optional)
- 1 teaspoon butter or coconut oil (optional, for extra richness)

Calories:	189
Protein:	2 grams
Carbohydrates:	34 grams
Fat:	6 grams
Fiber:	4 grams

Instructions:

1. Preheat your oven to 375°F (190°C).
2. Core the apple, leaving the bottom intact to create a small well for the filling. Peel a thin layer of skin around the top for even baking.
3. In a small bowl, mix the cinnamon, maple syrup (if using), nuts, and raisins. Spoon the mixture into the center of the apple. Top with a small dab of butter or coconut oil, if desired.
4. Place the apple in a small baking dish. Add a splash of water (about 2 tablespoons) to the dish to prevent sticking and create steam. Bake for 25-30 minutes, or until the apple is tender and can be easily pierced with a fork.
5. Let the baked apple cool slightly before serving. Enjoy on its own or with a dollop of Greek yogurt or whipped cream.

Avocado Chocolate Mousse

5 minutes

Ingredients:

- 1/4 large avocado
- 1 tablespoon unsweetened cocoa powder
- 1 tablespoon maple syrup or honey
- 1 tablespoon unsweetened almond milk
- 1/4 teaspoon vanilla extract (optional)

Calories:	160
Protein:	2 grams
Carbohydrates:	17 grams
Fat:	10 grams
Fiber:	5 grams

Instructions:

1. In a small food processor or blender, combine the avocado, cocoa powder, maple syrup, almond milk, and vanilla extract. Blend until smooth and creamy.
2. If the mousse is too thick, add a small splash of almond milk and blend again until it reaches your desired consistency.
3. Transfer the mousse to a small dish or ramekin. Serve immediately or chill in the refrigerator for a firmer texture.

Optional Toppings:

Garnish with fresh berries, a dollop of whipped cream, or a sprinkle of grated dark chocolate.

Coconut Macaroons

25 minutes

Serving: 1 (makes ~3 small macaroons)

Ingredients:

- 1/4 cup shredded unsweetened coconut
- 1 large egg white (use half if making a small batch)
- 1 teaspoon honey or maple syrup
- 1/4 teaspoon vanilla extract (optional)
- Pinch of salt

Calories:	95
Protein:	2 grams
Carbohydrates:	8 grams
Fat:	6 grams
Fiber:	2 grams

Instructions:

1. Preheat your oven to 325°F (160°C). Line a baking sheet with parchment paper or a silicone baking mat.
2. In a small bowl, combine the shredded coconut, egg white, honey, vanilla extract (if using), and a pinch of salt. Mix until well combined and sticky.
3. Use a tablespoon or your hands to form the mixture into small balls or mounds. Place them on the prepared baking sheet, spacing them slightly apart.
4. Bake in the preheated oven for 12-15 minutes, or until the tops are lightly golden.
5. Allow the macaroons to cool on the baking sheet for 5 minutes before transferring them to a wire rack to cool completely. Enjoy as a snack or dessert.

Honey Almond Rice Pudding

30 minutes

Ingredients:

- 1/4 cup cooked white or brown rice
- 1/2 cup almond milk
- 1 teaspoon honey
- 1/4 teaspoon vanilla extract
- Pinch of salt

Calories:	140
Protein:	3 grams
Carbohydrates:	27 grams
Fat:	2 grams
Fiber:	1 grams

Instructions:

1. In a small saucepan, combine the cooked rice, almond milk, honey, vanilla extract, and a pinch of salt.
2. Place the saucepan over medium heat. Cook the mixture, stirring frequently, until it begins to thicken and becomes creamy (about 15-20 minutes).
3. If the pudding is too thick, add a splash of almond milk to reach your desired consistency.
4. Transfer the pudding to a serving bowl. Top with optional sliced almonds, a sprinkle of cinnamon, or fresh fruit for extra flavor and texture. Serve warm or chilled.

Lemon Coconut Energy Balls

25 minutes

Ingredients:

- 2 tablespoons rolled oats
- 1 tablespoon shredded coconut
- 1 teaspoon almond butter
- 1/4 teaspoon lemon zest
- 1/2 teaspoon honey
- 1/2 teaspoon lemon juice

Calories:	75
Protein:	2 grams
Carbohydrates:	9 grams
Fat:	3 grams
Fiber:	1 grams

Instructions:

1. In a small bowl, mix together the rolled oats, shredded coconut, almond butter, lemon zest, honey, and lemon juice. Stir until the mixture is sticky and holds together.
2. Using your hands, roll the mixture into 2 small balls.
3. Place the balls in the refrigerator for at least 20 minutes to firm up.
4. Enjoy immediately or store in the refrigerator for up to 3 days.

Sweet Potato Brownies

30 minutes

Serving: 4 (makes 4 small brownies)

Ingredients:

- 1/2 cup mashed sweet potato (cooked and peeled)
- 2 tablespoons cocoa powder
- 1/4 cup almond flour
- 2 tablespoons maple syrup
- 1 large egg
- 1/4 teaspoon vanilla extract (optional)
- 1/4 teaspoon baking powder (optional, for fluffier brownies)
- Pinch of salt

Calories:	120
Protein:	3 grams
Carbohydrates:	16 grams
Fat:	5 grams
Fiber:	2 grams

Instructions:

1. Preheat your oven to 350°F (175°C). Grease a small baking dish or line it with parchment paper.
2. In a mixing bowl, combine the mashed sweet potato, cocoa powder, almond flour, maple syrup, egg, vanilla extract (if using), baking powder, and salt. Stir until smooth and well combined.
3. Transfer the batter to the prepared baking dish and spread evenly.
4. Bake in the preheated oven for 20-25 minutes, or until a toothpick inserted into the center comes out clean.
5. Allow the brownies to cool in the pan for 10 minutes before cutting into squares. Serve warm or at room temperature.

Cinnamon Roll Baked Oatmeal

30 minutes

Ingredients:

- 1/2 cup rolled oats
- 1/2 cup milk
- 1/2 teaspoon cinnamon
- 1 teaspoon honey or maple syrup
- 1/4 teaspoon vanilla extract (optional)
- 1/4 teaspoon baking powder (optional, for fluffier texture)
- Pinch of salt

Calories:	190
Protein:	6 grams
Carbohydrates:	30 grams
Fat:	3 grams
Fiber:	4 grams

Instructions:

1. Preheat your oven to 375°F (190°C). Grease a small ramekin or baking dish.
2. In a mixing bowl, combine the oats, milk, cinnamon, sweetener, vanilla extract, baking powder, and salt. Stir until well combined.
3. Pour the mixture into the prepared baking dish, spreading it evenly.
4. Bake in the preheated oven for 20-25 minutes, or until the oatmeal is set and lightly golden on top.
5. Let it cool slightly before serving. Add optional toppings for extra flavor, like a drizzle of cream cheese glaze (mix cream cheese, powdered sugar, and milk), chopped nuts, or a sprinkle of extra cinnamon.

Peach Crisp

25 minutes

Ingredients:

- 1 medium peach, sliced
- 2 tablespoons rolled oats
- 1 teaspoon honey
- 1/2 teaspoon cinnamon
- 1/2 teaspoon coconut oil or butter (optional)
- Pinch of salt

Calories:	190
Protein:	6 grams
Carbohydrates:	30 grams
Fat:	3 grams
Fiber:	4 grams

Instructions:

1. Preheat your oven to 375°F (190°C). Grease a small ramekin or oven-safe dish.
2. Toss the sliced peach with a pinch of cinnamon and salt. Spread the peaches evenly in the prepared dish.
3. In a small bowl, mix the rolled oats, honey, remaining cinnamon, and coconut oil or butter (if using) until crumbly.
4. Sprinkle the oat mixture evenly over the peaches. Bake for 18-20 minutes, or until the topping is golden brown and the peach juices are bubbling.
5. Let cool slightly before serving. Enjoy as is or with a dollop of Greek yogurt or a scoop of vanilla ice cream.

12-Week Meal Plan

Welcome to the **Good Energy 12-Week Meal Plan**! This carefully designed program is your guide to balanced, nutritious eating that boosts your energy, sustains your productivity, and supports your overall well-being. With a variety of delicious recipes, this plan ensures you enjoy every meal while fueling your body with the nutrients it needs.

Why This Plan is Great

- **Variety and Balance**: Each week is crafted with a mix of energizing breakfasts, satisfying lunches, wholesome dinners, and snacks to keep you feeling full and focused.

- **Efficiency**: Meals are easy to prepare, making this plan ideal for busy individuals looking for convenient, healthful options.

- **Flexibility**: The recipes cater to diverse tastes and dietary needs, offering options for everyone.

- **Structured Grocery Lists**: Each week's meal plan is accompanied by a categorized grocery list for hassle-free shopping.

This meal plan is your roadmap to better energy and nutrition. Start today and enjoy the journey to a healthier, more vibrant you!

Week 1

	Breakfast	Morning snack	Lunch	Afternoon Snack	Dinner
Day 1	Orange & Carrot Sunrise Smoothie	Apple Slices with Almond Butter	Taco Salad	Fruit & Nut Bar	Avocado Chicken Salad Bowl
Day 2	Almond Butter & Banana Toast	Cottage Cheese with Sunflower Seeds	Baked Chicken Parmesan with Greens Salad	Whole-Grain Crackers & Cheese	Italian-Style Stuffed Zucchini with Herbs
Day 3	Tropical Energizer Smoothie	String Cheese & Sliced Bell Pepper	Teriyaki Shrimp Stir-Fry	Banana & Peanut Butter	Mediterranean Baked Chicken with Olives and Tomatoes
Day 4	Orange & Carrot Sunrise Smoothie	Celery Sticks with Peanut Butter	Turkey & Sweet Potato Skillet	Rice Cakes with Avocado	Lemon Herb Lamb Chops with Steamed Broccoli
Day 5	Pumpkin Pie Oatmeal	Whole-Grain Crackers & Cheese	Grilled Veggie Sandwich	Greek Yogurt with Berries	Grilled Mahi-Mahi with Pineapple Salsa
Day 6	Green Power Smoothie	Mini Caprese Skewers	Mediterranean Lentil Salad	Almond Butter & Banana Rice Cake	Garlic and Lemon Chicken over Cauliflower Rice
Day 7	Turmeric Golden Oats	Hard-Boiled Egg & Spinach	Mediterranean Veggie Wrap	Cottage Cheese with Sunflower Seeds	Lemon Garlic Shrimp with Zoodles

Week 2

	Breakfast	**Morning snack**	**Lunch**	**Afternoon Snack**	**Dinner**
Day 8	Fruit & Nut Quinoa Bowl	Mini Veggie Wrap	Mushroom & Spinach Sauté	Celery Sticks with Peanut Butter	Tofu and Bell Pepper Stir-Fry with Ginger Soy Sauce
Day 9	Tomato & Avocado Toast	Apple & Cheese Slices	Peanut Noodles	Turkey & Cheese Roll-Ups	Lentil and Vegetable Stew
Day 10	Greek Yogurt & Berry Bowl	Turkey & Cheese Roll-Ups	Chicken & Spinach Pasta in Tomato Cream Sauce	Dark Chocolate & Almonds	Lemon Dill Tofu Bowl with Spinach
Day 11	Quinoa Breakfast Bowl	Greek Yogurt Parfait	Tuna Salad Sandwich	Greek Yogurt Parfait	Zucchini Noodles with Bolognese Sauce
Day 12	Apple Cinnamon Oatmeal	Cucumber & Hummus Sandwich	Sausage & Veggie Skillet	Mini Veggie Wrap	Sautéed Cabbage with White Beans and Garlic
Day 13	Tomato & Avocado Toast	Cottage Cheese & Peach Slices	Creamy Tomato Basil Soup	Apple Slices with Almond Butter	Sheet Pan Shrimp with Zucchini and Bell Peppers
Day 14	Cinnamon Raisin Oatmeal	Roasted Red Pepper Hummus with Pita Chips	Roasted Beet & Goat Cheese Salad	Cottage Cheese & Crushed Walnuts	Pork Tenderloin with Sautéed Spinach

Week 3

	Breakfast	Morning snack	Lunch	Afternoon Snack	Dinner
Day 15	Scrambled Eggs with Spinach & Feta	Edamame	Caprese Salad	Avocado & Tuna Salad	Sautéed Beef with Bell Peppers and Snap Peas
Day 16	Sautéed Veggies & Egg Bowl	Greek Yogurt with Honey & Walnuts	Southwest Beef Bowl	Apple & Cheese Slices	Chicken Stir-Fry with Bok Choy and Carrots
Day 17	Hummus & Veggie Toast	Baby Carrots with Ranch Greek Yogurt Dip	Chicken & Spinach with Tomato Sauce	Hard-Boiled Egg & Cherry Tomatoes	Balsamic Glazed Steak with Roasted Zucchini
Day 18	Classic Nut & Berry Oatmeal	Applesauce with Cinnamon & Almonds	Beef & Bell Pepper Stir-Fry	Edamame	Turkey Lettuce Wraps with Shredded Carrots
Day 19	Sweet Potato & Black Bean Bowl	Fruit & Nut Bar	Mexican-Style Rice & Bean Casserole	Pear Slices with Ricotta Cheese	Blackened Catfish with Cabbage Slaw
Day 20	Fruit & Nut Quinoa Bowl	Cottage Cheese & Crushed Walnuts	Baked Cod with Garlic and Herbs on Quinoa	Cucumber & Hummus Sandwich	Spicy Beef and Cauliflower Rice Bowl
Day 21	Sautéed Veggies & Egg Bowl	Oatmeal Muffin	Zucchini & Chickpea Sauté	Cottage Cheese with Berries	Chickpea Shawarma Bowl with Cucumber and Tzatziki

Week 4

	Breakfast	**Morning snack**	**Lunch**	**Afternoon Snack**	**Dinner**
Day 22	Berry Protein Smoothie	Nut & Seed Trail Mix	Chicken Tortilla Soup	Cottage Cheese & Chopped Green Apple	Baked Lemon Herb Salmon with Asparagus
Day 23	Almond Butter & Banana Toast	Rice Cakes with Avocado	Falafel Bowl	Hummus & Veggie Sticks	Cauliflower Fried Rice with Scrambled Eggs
Day 24	Savory Spinach & Egg Oatmeal	Cottage Cheese & Chopped Green Apple	Kale & Quinoa Salad	Simple Rice Cakes	Sweet Potato and Brussels Sprouts Hash
Day 25	Tahini & Berry Smoothie Bowl	Turkey Jerky & Almonds	Greek Salad	Turkey Jerky & Almonds	Thai Chicken and Cucumber Salad Bowl
Day 26	Greek Yogurt & Berry Bowl	Hummus & Veggie Sticks	Tomato Basil Pasta	Cottage Cheese & Peach Slices	Baked Turkey Meatballs with Green Beans
Day 27	Almond Butter Banana Bowl	Simple Rice Cakes	Italian-Inspired Eggplant Parmesan Casserole	Oatmeal Muffin	Grilled Shrimp and Pineapple Skewers
Day 28	Berry Almond Overnight Oats	Pear Slices with Ricotta Cheese	Baked Sweet Potatoes with Black Beans and Avocado	String Cheese & Sliced Bell Pepper	Roasted Brussels Sprouts and Carrots with Balsamic Glaze

Week 5

	Breakfast	Morning snack	Lunch	Afternoon Snack	Dinner
Day 29	Pumpkin Seed Butter & Raspberry Toast	Hard-Boiled Egg & Cherry Tomatoes	Spicy Black Bean Soup	Stuffed Mini Bell Peppers with Feta	Greek Bowl with Chicken, Cucumber, and Tzatziki
Day 30	Matcha Green Smoothie	Stuffed Mini Bell Peppers with Feta	Chicken Caesar Salad	Sliced Bell Pepper with Guacamole	Mediterranean Shrimp Bowl with Olives and Feta
Day 31	Oatmeal Smoothie	Cottage Cheese with Berries	Potato Leek Soup	Baby Carrots with Ranch Greek Yogurt Dip	Lemon Dill Trout with Steamed Green Beans
Day 32	Pumpkin Spice Smoothie	Almond Butter & Banana Rice Cake	Falafel & Hummus Wrap	Mini Caprese Skewers	Spaghetti Squash with Marinara and Mushrooms
Day 33	Cottage Cheese & Fruit Bowl	Avocado & Tuna Salad	Cashew Chicken Stir-Fry with Cauliflower Rice	Greek Yogurt with Honey & Walnuts	Cod with Cherry Tomatoes and Fresh Basil
Day 34	Matcha Green Smoothie	Sliced Bell Pepper with Guacamole	Eggplant & Tomato Bake	Roasted Red Pepper Hummus with Pita Chips	Lemon Dill Baked Cod with Baby Potatoes
Day 35	Chocolate Banana Oatmeal	Banana & Peanut Butter	Greek Chicken Bowl	Hard-Boiled Egg & Spinach	Mediterranean Eggplant and Greek Yogurt Bowl

Sophie Marigold

Week 6

	Breakfast	Morning snack	Lunch	Afternoon Snack	Dinner
Day 36	Peanut Butter Banana Smoothie	Dark Chocolate & Almonds	Stuffed Bell Peppers	Nut & Seed Trail Mix	Tilapia with Roasted Brussels Sprouts
Day 37	Tahini & Berry Smoothie Bowl	Greek Yogurt with Berries	Mediterranean Chickpea Bowl	Applesauce with Cinnamon & Almonds	Mushroom and Spinach Sauté over Rice
Day 38	Peanut Butter & Banana Oatmeal	Almond Butter & Banana Rice Cake	Pesto Chicken Pasta	Pear Slices with Ricotta Cheese	Quinoa and Black Bean Stuffed Bell Peppers
Day 39	Overnight Chia Oats	Applesauce with Cinnamon & Almonds	Butternut Squash & Apple Soup	Cottage Cheese & Peach Slices	Miso Glazed Salmon with Steamed Bok Choy
Day 40	Almond Butter Banana Bowl	Turkey & Cheese Roll-Ups	Spinach & Strawberry Salad	Cottage Cheese & Crushed Walnuts	Greek Yogurt, Cucumber, and Quinoa Bowl with Mint
Day 41	Avocado & Chickpea Bowl	Cucumber & Hummus Sandwich	Zoodles with Marinara	Greek Yogurt Parfait	Shrimp and Mango Salad with Lime
Day 42	Ricotta & Berry Toast	Cottage Cheese & Crushed Walnuts	Turkey & Avocado Wrap	Nut & Seed Trail Mix	Sautéed Spinach and Mushroom Cauliflower Rice Bowl

Week 7

	Breakfast	Morning snack	Lunch	Afternoon Snack	Dinner
Day 43	Avocado Berry Blast Smoothie	Apple & Cheese Slices	Broccoli & Chicken Alfredo	Oatmeal Muffin	Baked Chicken with Brussels Sprouts and Sweet Potatoes
Day 44	Apple Pie Smoothie	Baby Carrots with Ranch Greek Yogurt Dip	Classic Chicken Vegetable Soup	Cottage Cheese & Chopped Green Apple	Roasted Cauliflower Steaks with Garlic and Herbs
Day 45	Cauliflower Breakfast Bowl	Greek Yogurt with Honey & Walnuts	Lemon Garlic Shrimp Linguine	Whole-Grain Crackers & Cheese	Seared Scallops with Garlic and Lemon
Day 46	Cottage Cheese & Fruit Bowl	Apple Slices with Almond Butter	One-Pan Chicken & Veggie Skillet	Cucumber & Hummus Sandwich	Egg Roll in a Bowl with Ground Turkey
Day 47	Veggie Omelet	Edamame	Spicy Beef Ramen	Edamame	One-Pan Baked Sausage and Peppers
Day 48	Peanut Butter & Apple Toast	Whole-Grain Crackers & Cheese	Lentil & Vegetable Stew	Turkey & Cheese Roll-Ups	One-Pan Chicken and Mushroom Bake
Day 49	Mushroom & Avocado Toast	Cottage Cheese with Berries	Herb-Roasted Chicken Thighs with Green Beans	Banana & Peanut Butter	Garlic Rosemary Pork Chops with Green Beans

Week 8

	Breakfast	Morning snack	Lunch	Afternoon Snack	Dinner
Day 50	Smoked Salmon & Cucumber Toast	Avocado & Tuna Salad	Spicy Tuna Poke Bowl	Celery Sticks with Peanut Butter	Chipotle Chicken and Cauliflower Rice Bowl
Day 51	Egg & Spinach English Muffin	Hard-Boiled Egg & Spinach	Asian-Inspired Tofu Bowl	Stuffed Mini Bell Peppers with Feta	Herb-Roasted Chicken with Baby Carrots
Day 52	Spinach & Mushroom Scramble Bowl	Cottage Cheese with Sunflower Seeds	Buffalo Cauliflower Bowl	Mini Veggie Wrap	Grilled Chicken with Spinach and Cherry Tomato Salad
Day 53	Peanut Butter & Banana Roll-Up	Celery Sticks with Peanut Butter	Garlic Shrimp Pasta	Apple Slices with Almond Butter	Ratatouille with Chicken and Fresh Herbs
Day 54	Green Power Smoothie	Cottage Cheese & Chopped Green Apple	Tofu & Veggie Stir-Fry with Zoodles	Hard-Boiled Egg & Spinach	Buffalo Cauliflower Rice with Grilled Chicken
Day 55	Oatmeal Smoothie	Cottage Cheese & Peach Slices	Cheesy Cauliflower & Chicken Casserole	Rice Cakes with Avocado	Asian-Inspired Tofu and Cabbage Bowl
Day 56	Tropical Energizer Smoothie	Dark Chocolate & Almonds	Beef & Rice Skillet	Turkey Jerky & Almonds	Stuffed Portobello Mushrooms with Spinach and Feta

Week 9

	Breakfast	Morning snack	Lunch	Afternoon Snack	Dinner
Day 57	Protein Pancakes	Hard-Boiled Egg & Cherry Tomatoes	Tuscan White Bean Soup	Cottage Cheese with Sunflower Seeds	Pesto Zoodles with Cherry Tomatoes and Mozzarella
Day 58	Fig & Walnut Toast	Rice Cakes with Avocado	Quick Beef & Vegetable Stew	Hard-Boiled Egg & Cherry Tomatoes	Lemon Garlic Roasted Chicken Thighs with Asparagus
Day 59	Overnight Chia Oats	Oatmeal Muffin	BBQ Chicken Wrap	Avocado & Tuna Salad	Zucchini and Chickpea Sauté with Fresh Herbs
Day 60	Avocado Berry Blast Smoothie	Roasted Red Pepper Hummus with Pita Chips	Cheesy Broccoli & Quinoa Casserole	Greek Yogurt with Honey & Walnuts	Roasted Vegetable Bowl with Hummus Dressing
Day 61	Power Breakfast Bowl	Banana & Peanut Butter	Thai Coconut Curry Soup	Dark Chocolate & Almonds	Turkey and Zucchini Meatballs with Marinara Sauce
Day 62	Chocolate Banana Oatmeal	Stuffed Mini Bell Peppers with Feta	Avocado Shrimp Salad	Mini Caprese Skewers	Greek Chicken with Cucumber and Feta Salad
Day 63	Tofu Scramble	Fruit & Nut Bar	Roasted Veggie Quinoa Bowl	Almond Butter & Banana Rice Cake	Baked Eggplant Parmesan (light on cheese)

Week 10

	Breakfast	Morning snack	Lunch	Afternoon Snack	Dinner
Day 64	Hummus & Veggie Toast	Simple Rice Cakes	Pasta Primavera	Hummus & Veggie Sticks	Salmon and Avocado Bowl with Mixed Greens
Day 65	Greek Yogurt Parfait	Nut & Seed Trail Mix	Mexican Burrito Bowl	Apple & Cheese Slices	Broccoli and Almond Stir-Fry
Day 66	Smoked Salmon & Cucumber Toast	Turkey Jerky & Almonds	Buffalo Chicken Wrap	String Cheese & Sliced Bell Pepper	Parmesan-Crusted Cod with Broccoli
Day 67	Berry Almond Overnight Oats	Mini Caprese Skewers	Ginger Chicken Stir-Fry	Fruit & Nut Bar	Sautéed Veal with Kale and Butternut Squash
Day 68	Ricotta & Berry Toast	Hummus & Veggie Sticks	Chicken Caesar Wrap	Roasted Red Pepper Hummus with Pita Chips	Sweet Potato Noodles with Pesto and Cherry Tomatoes
Day 69	Scrambled Eggs with Spinach & Feta	Sliced Bell Pepper with Guacamole	Beef & Broccoli Stir-Fry	Sliced Bell Pepper with Guacamole	Chickpea and Spinach Stir-Fry
Day 70	Pumpkin Pie Oatmeal	Greek Yogurt with Berries	Tuna & Rice Casserole	Simple Rice Cakes	Eggplant and Tomato Bake with Parmesan

Week 11

	Breakfast	Morning snack	Lunch	Afternoon Snack	Dinner
Day 71	Peanut Butter & Banana Roll-Up	Pear Slices with Ricotta Cheese	BLT Sandwich	Greek Yogurt with Berries	Cauliflower Rice with Sautéed Shrimp
Day 72	Veggie Omelet	Mini Veggie Wrap	Garlic Shrimp & Asparagus	Cottage Cheese with Berries	Black Bean and Avocado Salad Bowl
Day 73	Pumpkin Seed Butter & Raspberry Toast	String Cheese & Sliced Bell Pepper	Avocado & Egg Sandwich	Baby Carrots with Ranch Greek Yogurt Dip	Roasted Cauliflower and Chickpea Bowl
Day 74	Greek Yogurt Parfait	Greek Yogurt Parfait	Baked Lemon Herb Salmon with Sweet Potato Mash	Applesauce with Cinnamon & Almonds	Garlic Butter Shrimp with Green Beans
Day 75	Quinoa Breakfast Bowl	Hard-Boiled Egg & Cherry Tomatoes	Asian Sesame Chicken Salad	Roasted Red Pepper Hummus with Pita Chips	Sweet Potato and Zucchini Bake with Garlic and Thyme
Day 76	Savory Spinach & Egg Oatmeal	Mini Veggie Wrap	Garlic Parmesan Roasted Brussels Sprouts	Pear Slices with Ricotta Cheese	Stuffed Zucchini Boats with Ground Turkey and Marinara
Day 77	Peanut Butter & Banana Oatmeal	Fruit & Nut Bar	Vegetable Fried Rice	Applesauce with Cinnamon & Almonds	Broccoli and Cheese Stuffed Chicken Breast

Week 12

	Breakfast	Morning snack	Lunch	Afternoon Snack	Dinner
Day 78	Berry Protein Smoothie	Avocado & Tuna Salad	Roasted Vegetable Medley with Baked Chicken	Greek Yogurt Parfait	Lemon Pepper Tilapia with Roasted Asparagus
Day 79	Smoked Salmon & Avocado Toast	Celery Sticks with Peanut Butter	Roasted Cauliflower with Tahini Drizzle and Couscous	Turkey Jerky & Almonds	Stuffed Zucchini Boats with Ground Turkey and Marinara
Day 80	Power Breakfast Bowl	Greek Yogurt with Berries	BBQ Chicken Bowl	Dark Chocolate & Almonds	Sweet Potato and Black Bean Skillet
Day 81	Fig & Walnut Toast	Greek Yogurt Parfait	Falafel Bowl	Apple Slices with Almond Butter	Parmesan-Crusted Cod with Broccoli
Day 82	Tofu Scramble	Sliced Bell Pepper with Guacamole	Pasta Primavera	Banana & Peanut Butter	Lemon Garlic Turkey Cutlets with Roasted Peppers
Day 83	Egg & Spinach English Muffin	Dark Chocolate & Almonds	Garlic Shrimp Pasta	Cottage Cheese & Crushed Walnuts	Cauliflower Rice with Sautéed Shrimp
Day 84	Cauliflower Breakfast Bowl	Banana & Peanut Butter	Zucchini & Chickpea Sauté	Hummus & Veggie Sticks	Roasted Brussels Sprouts and Carrots with Balsamic Glaze

BONUS 1

Lifestyle Tips for Lasting Energy

Eating well is essential for sustained energy, but your lifestyle choices also play a significant role in how energized you feel each day. Lasting energy comes from a combination of balanced nutrition, quality sleep, stress management, and physical activity. By making mindful adjustments in these areas, you can boost your resilience, focus, and vitality. Here are some lifestyle tips to help you maintain high energy levels and thrive in all areas of your life.

1. Prioritize Quality Sleep

Sleep is the foundation of lasting energy. While it might seem tempting to cut back on sleep to get more done, this often leads to reduced productivity and lower energy in the long run. Prioritizing sleep helps your body recharge, supports brain function, and strengthens your immune system.

- **Aim for 7-9 Hours of Sleep**: Most adults need between 7 and 9 hours of quality sleep per night. Find the amount that works best for you and create a bedtime routine to make it a priority.

- **Establish a Relaxing Routine**: Wind down before bed by disconnecting from screens, practicing relaxation techniques (like deep breathing or reading), or sipping a calming tea. Avoid caffeine, heavy meals, and intense exercise in the hours leading up to bedtime.

- **Create a Sleep-Friendly Environment**: Keep your bedroom cool, dark, and quiet. Consider using blackout curtains, earplugs, or a white noise machine to optimize your sleep environment.

2. Manage Stress Effectively

Chronic stress drains your energy and can leave you feeling mentally and physically exhausted. Managing stress is crucial for maintaining a stable, energized state of mind. By building resilience to stress, you'll protect your energy reserves and be better equipped to handle life's demands.

- **Practice Mindfulness**: Techniques like meditation, deep breathing, and yoga can help calm the mind and reduce stress. Taking even a few minutes each day to focus on your breath can significantly improve your ability to handle stress.

- **Prioritize Self-Care**: Schedule regular self-care activities that help you relax and recharge, such as taking a walk in nature, enjoying a hobby, or spending time with loved ones. Taking breaks throughout the day helps prevent burnout and maintains mental clarity.

- **Set Boundaries**: Learn to say no to tasks and commitments that don't serve you. Setting healthy boundaries at work and in personal relationships can free up energy for what truly matters and reduce unnecessary stress.

---

3. Stay Physically Active

Exercise isn't just beneficial for physical health – it also plays a crucial role in mental clarity, mood stability, and energy. Regular physical activity improves circulation, boosts endorphins, and helps regulate blood sugar levels, all of which contribute to sustained energy.

- **Find Movement You Enjoy**: Choose activities that you find enjoyable and energizing, whether that's walking, dancing, yoga, or strength training. Moving in a way you enjoy makes it easier to stay consistent.

- **Incorporate Short, Energizing Breaks**: Even brief physical activities, like a 10-minute walk or a quick stretch, can recharge your energy. Stand up, move around, and stretch during breaks to prevent fatigue and stay focused.

- **Aim for Consistency, Not Intensity**: You don't need intense workouts every day to feel energized. Focus on regular, moderate movement that fits into your routine without overwhelming you. Aim for at least 150 minutes of moderate exercise per week, as recommended by health experts.

---

4. Get Sunlight and Fresh Air

Exposure to natural light, especially in the morning, helps regulate your body's internal clock (circadian rhythm), which in turn supports better sleep and energy levels. Fresh air and time spent in nature also have restorative effects on the mind and body, boosting mood and vitality.

- **Morning Sunlight**: Try to get outside in the morning for at least 10-15 minutes. Sunlight exposure in the early part of the day helps regulate your circadian rhythm, which improves sleep quality and daytime energy.

- **Take Breaks Outdoors**: Incorporate short outdoor breaks into your day. Whether it's during lunch or between tasks, stepping outside for fresh air can help reduce stress and improve focus.

- **Consider Nature Walks**: Spending time in nature, like walking in a park or forest, has been shown to reduce stress and improve overall well-being. Even a brief walk in a natural setting can have positive effects on your energy and mood.

5. Maintain Balanced Blood Sugar

Energy isn't just about what you eat – it's also about how you maintain your blood sugar throughout the day. Blood sugar fluctuations can lead to energy crashes and mood swings, making it difficult to stay productive.

- **Eat at Regular Intervals**: Try not to skip meals or go long periods without eating. Aim to eat something every 3-4 hours to keep your blood sugar stable.

- **Choose Balanced Snacks**: When you need a snack, opt for something that combines protein, complex carbs, and healthy fats. Examples include apple slices with almond butter, Greek yogurt with berries, or hummus with veggies.

- **Limit Sugary Foods and Beverages**: Sugary snacks and drinks may provide a quick energy boost but are often followed by an energy crash. Prioritize whole, nutrient-dense foods that provide steady, sustained energy.

6. Create an Energizing Routine

Incorporating energizing habits into your daily routine can make a significant difference in how you feel. From the moment you wake up to the end of the day, simple practices can set the tone for sustained energy and focus.

- **Start Your Day Mindfully**: Begin the day with a glass of water, a nourishing breakfast, and a moment of calm. Avoid diving straight into screens or stressful tasks. Instead, try journaling, setting intentions, or practicing gratitude to start the day on a positive note.

- **Plan Ahead**: Preparing meals, snacks, and to-do lists in advance can save you time and mental energy. When you have a clear plan, it's easier to stay organized and focused, avoiding the energy drain that comes with decision fatigue.

- **Wind Down in the Evening**: Just as it's important to start your day mindfully, it's essential to end it with intention. Create a relaxing evening routine that allows you to transition from the demands of the day to restful sleep. Activities like reading, stretching, or taking a warm bath can help your mind and body unwind.

Putting It All Together

A Good Energy Diet goes beyond food – it's about creating a lifestyle that supports consistent, lasting energy. By prioritizing sleep, managing stress, staying active, getting sunlight, balancing blood sugar, and establishing energizing routines, you'll be better equipped to face each day with focus, vitality, and resilience.

As you move forward in this journey, remember that small changes add up. Start by incorporating one or two of these tips into your daily routine, and build from there. The goal is to create habits that feel natural and sustainable, supporting your energy and well-being every day.

BONUS 2

Meal Prep Tips and Different Solutions

Meal Prep Tips

Meal prepping is an essential strategy for anyone looking to maintain a Good Energy Diet. By preparing meals in advance, you can ensure that you always have nutritious options available, making it easier to stick to your healthy eating habits. Here are some practical meal prep tips to help you get started:

1. **Plan Your Meals**: Spend some time each week planning your meals. Consider what recipes you want to try, and make a shopping list based on those meals. Aim for a variety of proteins, grains, and vegetables to keep your meals exciting and balanced.

2. **Batch Cooking**: Prepare large quantities of key ingredients that you can use throughout the week. Cook a big batch of quinoa, brown rice, or lentils, and store them in the fridge. You can easily mix and match these bases with different proteins and vegetables to create quick meals.

3. **Use Clear Containers**: Invest in a set of clear, airtight containers for storing your prepped meals. This will make it easy to see what you have available, helping you make quicker choices when you're hungry.

4. **Label Everything**: Label your containers with the meal name and date it was prepared. This will help you keep track of freshness and encourage you to eat what you've already prepared.

5. **Keep Snacks Handy**: Pre-portion healthy snacks like cut-up veggies, fruit, or nut mixes in grab-and-go containers. This can help you avoid unhealthy snacking and keep your energy levels stable throughout the day.

6. **Prep Breakfast Ahead**: Overnight oats, smoothies, or chia puddings can be prepared the night before and stored in the fridge for quick breakfasts on busy mornings.

7. **Utilize Freezer Space**: If you have meals or ingredients that you won't use within the week, freeze them. Soups, stews, and pre-cooked proteins can be frozen and reheated for a quick meal.

By incorporating these meal prep strategies into your routine, you can simplify your week and ensure you always have healthy, energy-boosting meals at your fingertips.

Supplements for Energy

While a well-balanced diet should provide the nutrients you need for optimal energy levels, some individuals may find it beneficial to explore safe, evidence-based supplements. Here are a few common supplements to consider for energy support:

1. **B Vitamins**: B vitamins, particularly B12 and B6, play a crucial role in energy production. They help convert food into energy and support brain function. If you follow a vegetarian or vegan diet, you may need a B12 supplement, as this vitamin is primarily found in animal products.

2. **Magnesium**: Magnesium is essential for muscle function and energy production. It can help reduce fatigue and improve exercise performance. Foods rich in magnesium include nuts, seeds, and leafy green vegetables, but a supplement can be helpful if you're not getting enough through diet.

3. **Vitamin D**: Low levels of vitamin D can lead to fatigue and low energy levels. If you live in an area with limited sunlight exposure, consider getting your vitamin D levels checked and discuss supplementation with your healthcare provider.

4. **Iron**: Iron is crucial for oxygen transport in the blood. If you're experiencing fatigue and are at risk for iron deficiency (common in women and vegetarians), a supplement may be necessary. Foods rich in iron include red meat, lentils, and fortified cereals.

5. **Adaptogens**: Herbal supplements like ashwagandha, rhodiola, and ginseng are known as adaptogens, which may help the body adapt to stress and support energy levels. However, it's essential to research and consult with a healthcare professional before adding herbal supplements to your regimen.

Always consult with a healthcare provider before starting any new supplements, especially if you have pre-existing health conditions or are taking medications.

Common Pitfalls and Solutions

Maintaining energy levels throughout the day can be challenging, especially when faced with common pitfalls like afternoon slumps or cravings. Here are some troubleshooting tips and quick fixes to help you stay on track:

1. **Afternoon Slump**: If you find yourself feeling lethargic in the afternoon, consider the following:

   o **Snack Smart**: Choose a snack that combines protein and healthy fats, like nut butter on whole-grain toast or a handful of nuts. This can provide a sustained energy boost.

   o **Hydration Check**: Dehydration can lead to fatigue. Keep a water bottle handy and aim to drink enough fluids throughout the day.

   o **Move Your Body**: A quick walk or stretching can help rejuvenate your energy levels. Even a few minutes of physical activity can increase blood flow and alertness.

2. **Cravings**: If you're struggling with cravings, try these strategies:

   o **Identify Triggers**: Keep a journal to track when cravings occur. Identifying patterns can help you address the underlying causes.

   o **Healthy Alternatives**: Have healthy options available to satisfy your cravings. For instance, if you're craving something sweet, reach for fresh fruit or a small piece of dark chocolate.

   o **Mindful Eating**: Practice mindfulness by paying attention to your hunger signals. Are you eating out of boredom or stress? Take a moment to assess whether you are truly hungry.

3. **Meal Timing**: Ensure you're eating at regular intervals throughout the day. Skipping meals can lead to energy crashes. Aim for three balanced meals with healthy snacks in between to maintain steady energy levels.

4. **Sleep Quality**: Poor sleep can significantly impact energy levels. Prioritize good sleep hygiene by establishing a consistent sleep schedule, creating a restful environment, and minimizing screen time before bed.

By implementing these tips and solutions, you can navigate common pitfalls and maintain high energy levels throughout the day, ultimately supporting your Good Energy Diet journey.

Made in the USA
Las Vegas, NV
22 December 2024

15149054R00109